The Dressmaker's Handbook

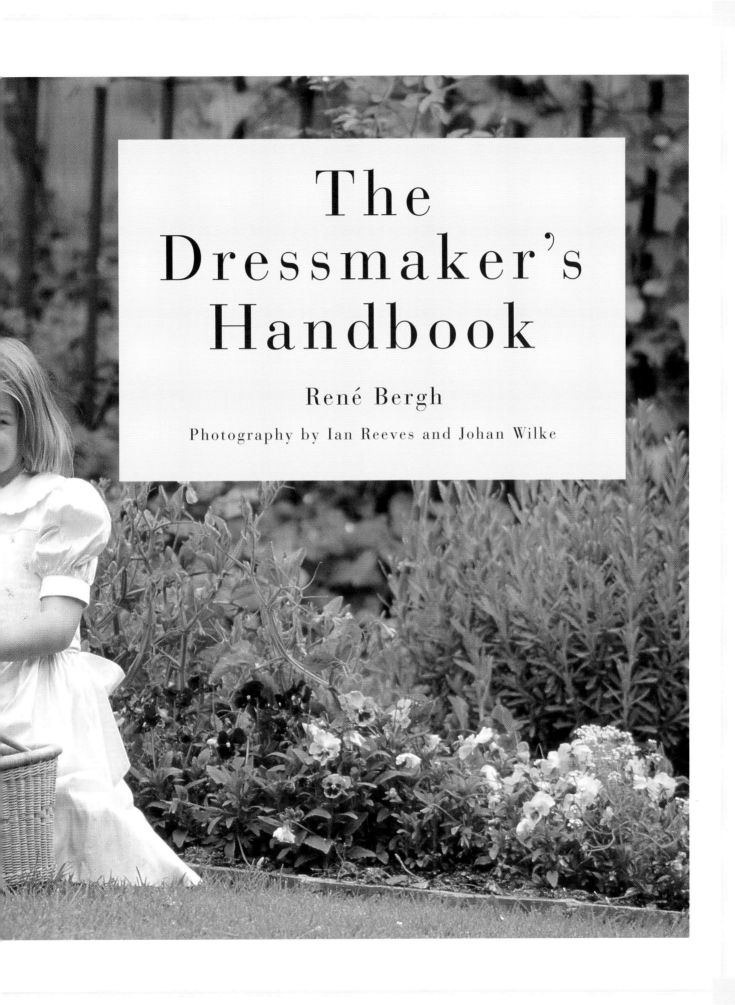

The Dressmaker's Handbook

René Bergh

Photography by Ian Reeves and Johan Wilke

Author's Acknowledgments

I am indebted to many people for their assistance and support, and extend my sincere thanks to: Dave Snook for his beautiful illustrations and hours of sheer dedication; Jenni Rabinowitz for her warmth, understanding and tireless effort; Ian Reeves, Johan Wilke and his assitant Ockert Fourie for their superb photographs; Debbie Cochrane and Joanne McCullough for hair and make-up; the team of models – Emma Mitchell, Marie-Therese and Vanessa Waibel, Kate Ibbotson, Taryn Möller and my son, Justin; Stephanie Waibel, Ute of Stock Exchange and all the various people whose wardrobes we scratched through; Catherine Moore and Denise Woodgate for the use of their dummies; Iona Bennie and my mother, Eunice Duffett, for the use of their sewing equipment; Wendy and Keith Maxwell, Glenda and Gavin Younge, and Mr and Mrs Youngelson for allowing us to invade their beautiful homes at short notice; the publishing team – Linda de Villiers, Petal Palmer, Christabel Hardacre, Thea Coetzee and especially Odette Marais – for all their hard work; and ultimately to my children, Justin and Hayden, for their moral support and allowing me to work in peace.

First published in 1998 by
New Holland (Publishers) Ltd
London • Cape Town • Sydney • Singapore

24 Nutford Place
London W1H 6DQ
United Kingdom

80 McKenzie Street
Cape Town 8001
South Africa

3/2 Aquatic Drive
Frenchs Forest, NSW 2086
Australia

ISBN 1 85368 710 3 (h/b)
ISBN 1 85974 016 2 (p/b)

Editor Thea Coetzee
Concept Design Petal Palmer
Designer Christabel Hardacre
Design Assistant Lellyn Creamer
Illustrator Dave Snook
Photographers Ian Reeves and Johan Wilke
Stylists Jenni Rabinowitz and Odette Marais

Reproduction by Unifoto (Pty) Ltd, Cape Town
Printed and bound by Tien Wah Press (Pte) Ltd, Singapore

INTRODUCTION

Anyone can produce haute couture. All you need is a fundamental knowledge of sewing and the ability to operate a sewing machine. Designer patterns are available commercially, and in the first section of this book you will be shown how to select the pattern that is best suited to your specific requirements. You may need to alter these patterns, but this is not as daunting as it first appears.

The next step is to select fabric of which the texture and colour is not only suitable to the style but will also enhance your appearance. The correct cutting procedure is of vital importance. John Galliano's trademark is the bias-cut slinky dress and, however unforgiving to the belly and hips, it is a challenge that most women seem to relish.

Following professional advice regarding techniques and finishes can be crucial to the end product. I've included some foolproof short cuts and useful designer tips throughout this book. Wherever you look, couturiers can be identified: Balenciaga's jackets are distinguished by the way their sleeves are set in; Chanel's by their cardigan shape; Gaultier disguises the rigidity of strict tailoring with his hip urban attire; Armani has removed the structure from the jacket and replaced it with more flexibility. These are just some of the techniques that have become their signatures.

The final construction of a garment requires the discipline to follow the correct procedure. As Donna Karan advised American *Vogue*: 'To me, the future is all about personal style, not designer dictates. My role is to offer women the freedom and tools to pull it together in a completely modern, sexy way – with simplified pieces that are timeless, luxurious, and flexible enough to go day into evening. This is not about a season; it's about everything I stand for. Building a wardrobe.' I hope this book will be of great assistance and an inspiration to you as you create your wardrobe.

CONTENTS

PREPARATION

Whether you are sewing a simple T-shirt or a tailored jacket, there are certain essential tools that will be required to accomplish the task. A well-stocked and organized workroom will facilitate this. Select a pattern that complements your figure and alter it where necessary. Christian Lacroix, known for his superb colour sense and his deep understanding of the finest fabrics, should be an inspiration when choosing your fabric. Fusing the appropriate interfacing also needs careful consideration. Pattern pieces should be placed economically (yet in accordance with the grain lines) and the pattern matched where necessary.

EQUIPMENT REQUIRED

Although it is possible to make a garment with very few tools, a limited sewing kit will certainly slow you down and add a lot of frustration to the task. Basic sewing is divided into these processes: measuring, marking, cutting, stitching (either by hand or by machine) and pressing. The tools represented on these pages are essential for simplifying the steps and will result in a professional finish.

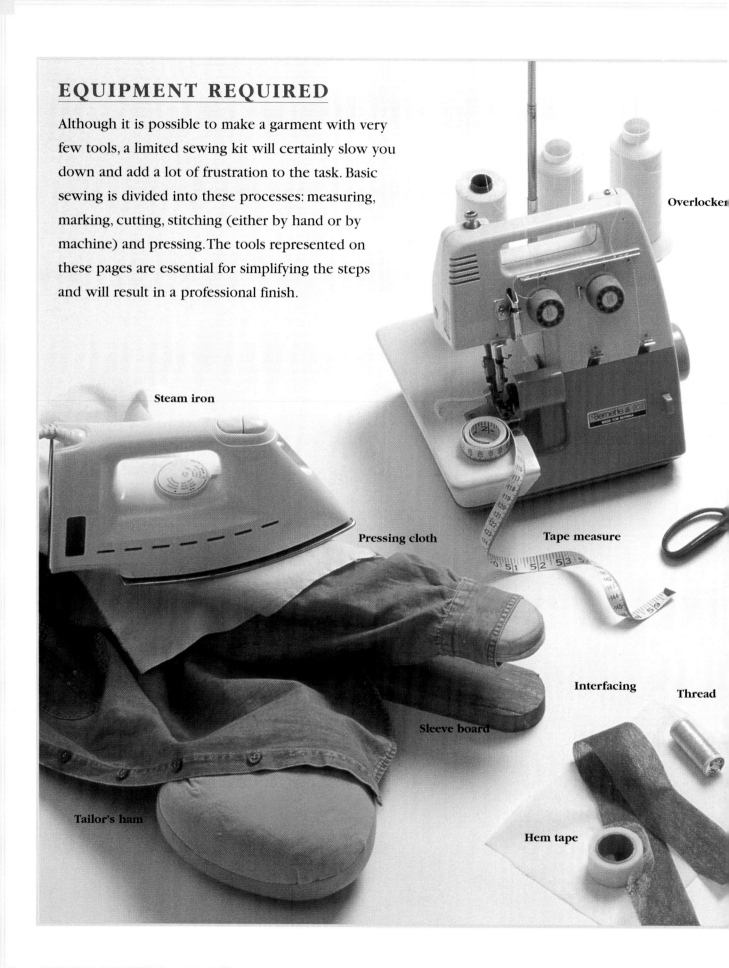

Overlocker

Steam iron

Pressing cloth

Tape measure

Interfacing

Thread

Sleeve board

Tailor's ham

Hem tape

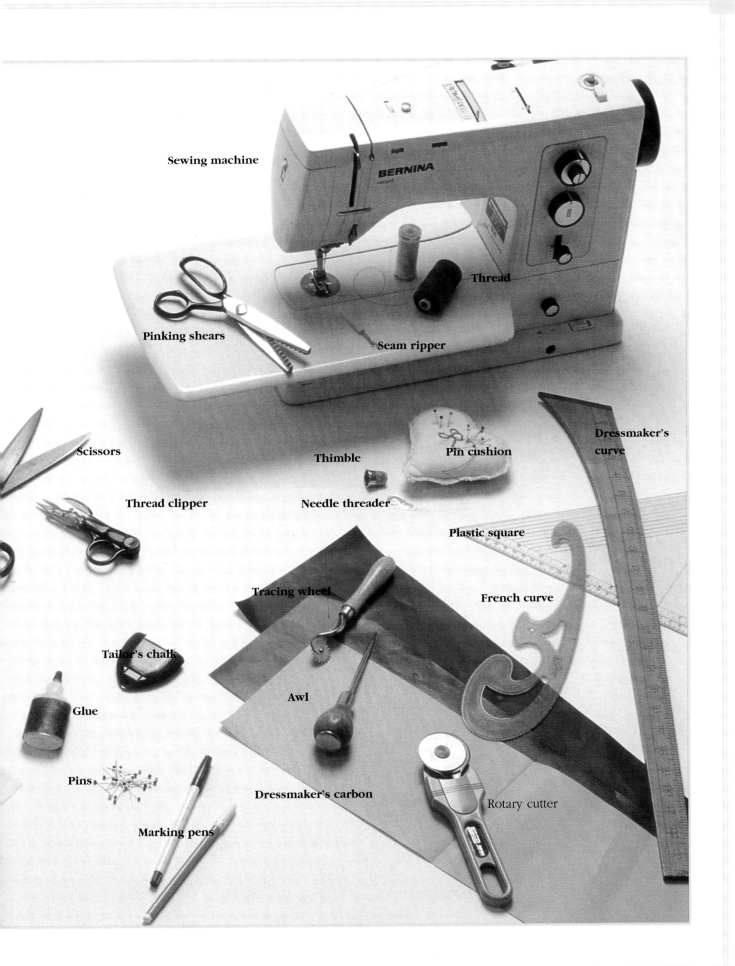

Sewing machine

Thread

Pinking shears

Seam ripper

Scissors

Thimble

Pin cushion

Dressmaker's curve

Thread clipper

Needle threader

Plastic square

French curve

Tracing wheel

Tailor's chalk

Awl

Glue

Pins

Dressmaker's carbon

Rotary cutter

Marking pens

TAKING MEASUREMENTS

Taking comprehensive, accurate body measurements is the key to a good fit. To achieve this, wear your usual undergarments or a body stocking and preferably get a friend to measure you. Use a firm tape measure that will not stretch. Having completed this task, determine your figure type and compare your body measurements with those on the commercial pattern charts to decide which is the closest match. Adjustments can be made to these patterns, or you can construct your own pattern. Commercial patterns are divided into figure types: Young junior/teen, Junior petite, Junior, Miss petite, Miss, Half-size, Woman, Maternity.

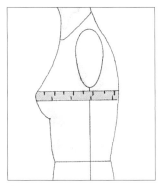

BUST

Around the fullest part – about 5 cm (2 in) below the armhole.

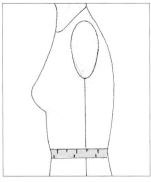

WAIST

A fairly snug measure-ment around the waist.

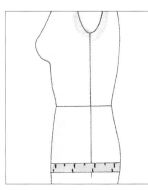

HIP

Around the fullest part – about 18 cm (7 in) below the waist.

CENTRE BACK

Back waist length, from the nape of the neck to the waist.

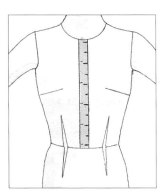

CENTRE FRONT

From the base of the neck to the waist.

BACK SHOULDER HEIGHT

From the shoulder at the neck to the waist.

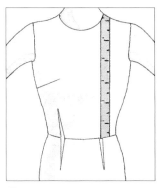

FRONT SHOULDER HEIGHT

From the shoulder at the neck to the waist.

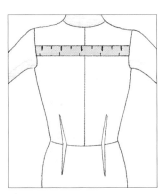

ACROSS BACK

From armhole to armhole about 12 cm (5 in) down from the neck.

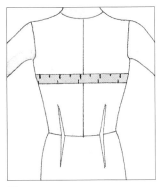

FULL BACK

From side seam to side seam about 5 cm (2 in) below the armhole.

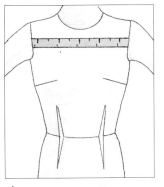

ACROSS FRONT

From armhole to armhole about 7 cm (3 in) down from the neck.

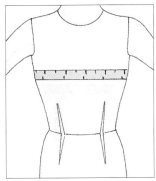

FULL FRONT

Across the bust from side seam to side seam 5 cm (2 in) below the armhole.

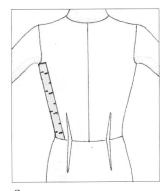

SIDE SEAM

From the armhole to the waist.

SHOULDER

From the neck to the sleeve crown.

NECK CIRCUMFERENCE

A fairly loose measurement around the base of the neck.

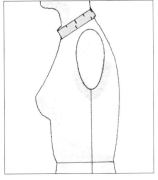

CROTCH

Taken in a sitting position from the waist to the chair.

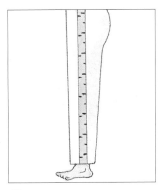

OUTSIDE LEG

From the waist over the hip to the ankle.

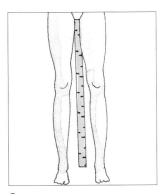

INSIDE LEG

From the crotch to the inside ankle.

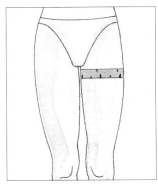

THIGH

Around the fullest part of the thigh.

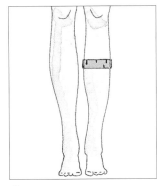

CALF

Around the fullest part of the calf.

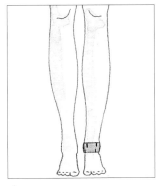

ANKLE

Around the ankle.

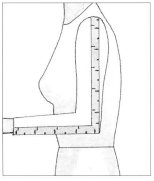

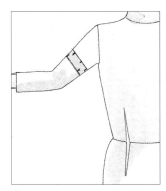

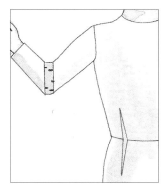

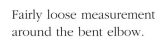

OVERARM

From sleeve crown round bent elbow to wrist.

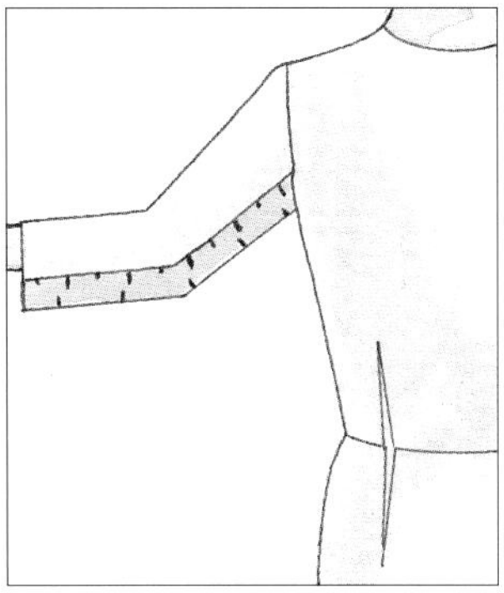

UNDERARM

From the bottom of the armhole to the wrist.

BICEP

Around the fullest part of the upper arm.

ELBOW

Fairly loose measurement around the bent elbow.

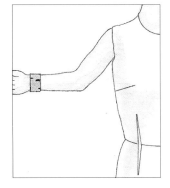

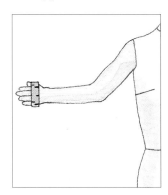

FITTED WRIST

A fairly loose measurement around the wrist.

LOOSE WRIST

With fingers together, a fairly snug measurement around the broadest part of the hand.

The measurements in this chart are taken from average bodies.
The sizes range from 32 to 46 (10 to 24). Use this as a guide to your particular size.

Sizes	32	UK 10	US 8	34	UK 12	US 10	36	UK 14	US 12	38	UK 16	US 14	40	UK 18	US 16	42	UK 20	US 18	44	UK 22	US 20	46	UK 24	US 22
	CM		IN	CM		IN	CM		IN	CM		IN	CM		IN	CM		IN	CM		IN	CM		IN
Bust	82		32	87		34	92		36	97		38	102		40	107		42	112		44	117		46
Waist	61		24	66		26	71		28	76		30	81		32	86		34	91		36	96		38
Hip	87		34	92		36	97		38	102		40	107		42	112		44	117		46	122		48
Neck	36.5		14½	37.5		15	38.5		15½	40		16	41.5		16½	43		17	44.5		17½	46		18
Centre back	41.5		16¼	42		16½	42.5		16¾	43.5		17¼	44		17½	45		17¾	45.5		18	46		18
Front shoulder height	42		16½	43.5		17¼	45		17¾	46		18	47.5		18¾	48.5		19¼	50		19¾	51.5		20¼
Shoulder	12		4¾	12.5		5	13		5¼	13		5¼	13.5		5½	13.5		5½	14		5¾	14.5		5¾
Overarm	58.5		23	59		23¼	59.5		23½	60		23½	60.5		23¾	61		24	61.5		24¼	62		24½
Bicep	28		11	29		11½	30		12	32		12½	34		13½	36		14¼	38		15	40		16
Wrist	15.5		6	16		6¼	16.5		6½	17.5		6¾	18		7	18.5		7¼	19		7½	19.5		7¾
Outside leg	109		43	110		43¼	111		43¾	112		44	113		44½	114		45	115		45¼	116		45¾

PATTERN SELECTION

To achieve a harmonious effect which is pleasing to the eye, you have to apply the basic principles of design. Proportion requires all parts to be related to one another in size, length and bulk, and balance is achieved by maintaining equal amounts of interest in either direction from the focal point. The eye should move smoothly across the garment and be drawn to the main design feature.

Even though current fashion trends as well as personal preferences will influence your choice of design, make a realistic analysis of yourself and decide which features should be emphasized and which need to be camouflaged. Various illusions can be created by artfully combining line, detail, texture and colour. Bear in mind that fabric patterns have a line and direction of their own and should be carefully considered when making your decision. Suffice it to say that colour and fabric also play an important role.

Silhouettes

The outer lines of a garment form its silhouette. There are two basic silhouettes, namely the rectangle and the triangle. A fitted garment will emphasize the body's contours, whereas the less fitted shape will detract from the body and make the garment's silhouette more dominant, as will fewer seams or details. A crisp fabric moulds the garment shape whereas a soft one tends to outline and emphasize the body shape.

Rectangle

This silhouette will accentuate height and tends to have a slimming effect. A boxy shape will, however, diminish height. Seams, details and fabric choice will modify both these shapes.

Triangle

An A-line shape counteracts broad shoulders and a large bust. A V-line shape, having its width at the top, will help to balance a wide hipline but will tend to diminish height. In both cases, by elongating the triangle, an illusion of height can be achieved.

These are examples of rectangular silhouettes

Here are some typical triangular silhouettes

Structural lines

Another dimension can be added to a silhouette by skilfully adding lines within a design. Illusions and diversions can be created that will help to establish balance and give good proportion to the figure.

Vertical

Vertical lines usually create the illusion of height and slimness, but when repeated at even intervals, they can make the figure appear wider and even shorter by drawing the eye from side to side.

Horizontal

When a horizontal line is used at the waist, it tends to diminish the height by seemingly cutting the garment in half. However, when used as a yoke seam or at the hip, the focus falls on the smaller area of the garment, thus appearing to lengthen the other area. When two horizontal lines are used together, the width is emphasized.

Diagonal

Depending on their length and angle, diagonals can add both height and width. A long diagonal will produce an elongated feeling, whereas a short one will create the illusion of width by adding focus to that area. Diagonals should move from left to right for a pleasing effect.

Curved

Curved lines emphasize the curves of the body. They fulfil the same basic function of illusion as straight lines. In some cases, by curving a straight line, the visual effect will be softened, thus making the design more graceful. Curves ultimately add roundness and can create a look of greater weight.

Commercial patterns

Most commercial pattern companies have basic patterns for the home dressmaker. They are sold in fabric stores and are listed in catalogues. Information about measuring, adjusting, sewing and fitting is included with each pattern. Choose a suitable pattern that coincides closely with your body measurements (*see* page 14), and make the necessary alterations as described on pages 17–19.

Butterick, McCall's, Simplicity and Vogue have developed their basic patterns using a standardized measurement chart published by the National Bureau of Standards. However, there are differences in the fit of their patterns. New Look and Style have identical fitting lines. Butterick and Vogue also have identical fitting lines.

Vertical Lines

Horizontal Lines

Special features

Short centre front due to head tilting forward
New Look, Style and Burda draft the lowest
centre front necklines.

Broad shoulders New Look, Style and
Simplicity draft patterns with the longest
shoulder seam lines.

Wide back New Look, Style and Burda draft
the widest backs.

Back more erect or more rounded Burda
drafts the largest dart for contouring around
the upper back.

*More than a 5 cm (2 in) difference between
the chest and bust measurements* New Look
and Style have built in the most fitting ease
through the bust; McCall's offers the least.

Bust point high or low Burda and Simplicity
have higher bust points; New Look and Style
have lower bust points.

Wide or narrow spread bust McCall's and
Burda cater for a narrow spread; New Look
and Style have a wider spread.

Full ribcage and waist New Look, Style and
Burda are fuller through the waist and have
narrow waist darts.

Full hips and thighs New Look, Style and
Simplicity draft the most here; Vogue and
Butterick have the most slender drafts.

Full or thin arms New Look and Simplicity
draft the widest bicep; Burda drafts the least.

Multisize patterns
Most women's measurements do not correspond
exactly with one size. The commercial pattern
companies have therefore compiled multisize
patterns, having realized that figure variations need
a range of sizes to overcome this problem.

Adjusting and reinforcing commercial patterns
Enclosed in each commercial pattern envelope are
general instructions on measuring, adjusting, cutting
and sewing. It is advisable to read these before
attempting any adjustments. If the pattern needs
altering, it might be necessary to reinforce the thin
tissue paper to prevent tearing.

Shortening a pattern
Fold the pattern pieces along the adjustment lines to
form a tuck measuring half the amount that it needs
to be shortened. The total amount will be twice the
depth. Adjust the darts and side seams if necessary.

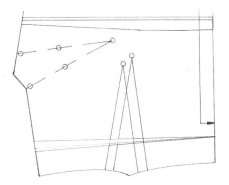

Lengthening a pattern
Cut the paper along the adjustment lines, place
graph or tissue paper underneath the pattern and
spread the required distance. Tape the paper
together, check all the dart placements and side
seams, and adjust if necessary.

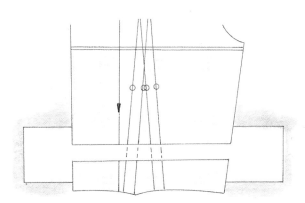

Increasing the bust

1 Draw a line through the centre of the waist dart and another through the side dart. These lines should intersect at the bust point. Draw another line from the bust point to the armhole, as illustrated.

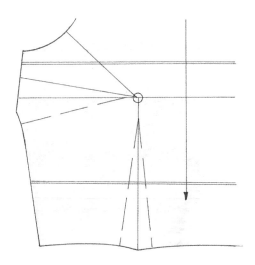

2 Slash the line from the waist through the bust point to the armhole. Ensure that the pattern still remains attached at the armhole. Slash the other line from the side seam to the bust point, making sure that all the pieces remain attached.

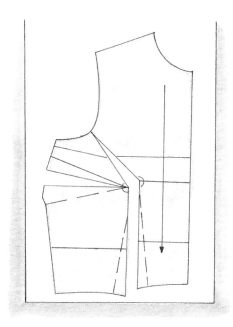

3 Place a piece of paper under the pattern and spread the pieces to the required measurement, as illustrated. Redraw the dart points (they should stop about 5 cm [2 in] away from the bust point) and extend the centre front length so that it corresponds with the new dart. Fold the dart and trim accordingly.

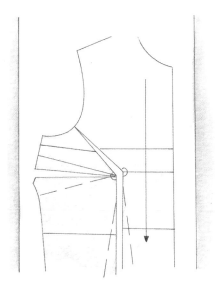

For more accuracy, seam allowances are excluded from these alterations and should be added afterwards. The standard industrial seam allowance is 1 cm ($^3/_8$ in), though commercial patterns usually allow 1.5 cm ($^5/_8$ in). Multisize fashion patterns only have cutting lines.

Trouser alterations

Swayback Lower the waist at the centre back, tapering it off to the side seams.

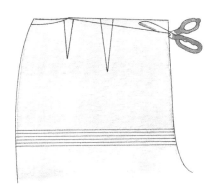

Protruding abdomens Raise the waist at the centre front, tapering it off to the side seams.

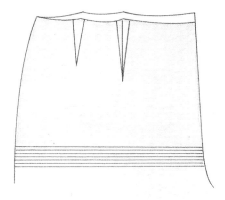

Full buttocks Extend the seam at the back crotch curve, tapering it off towards the knee.

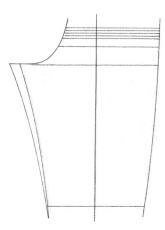

Flat buttocks Remove some of the inside seam at the back crotch curve, tapering off towards the knee.

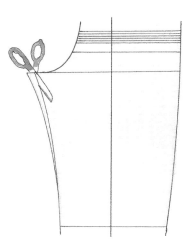

Wide thighs Extend the back and front crotch curves, tapering off towards the knees. Curve the outside side seams slightly at the thighs, tapering off towards the knees and hips.

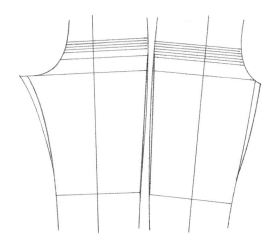

Thick waist and hips Extend the waistline, tapering off towards the hip at the side seams. Increase the waistband to correspond with the new measurement. This alteration will also apply to a skirt.

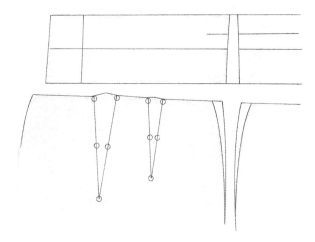

Any further adjustments can be done in a similar way. Stiff, non-woven interfacing can be fused onto the tissue pattern piece to stabilize it. Alternatively, the pattern piece can be traced onto firmer paper or cardboard.

FABRIC CHOICE

All fabrics are based on two types of fibres: natural fibres such as cotton, linen, wool and silk, and man-made fibres such as polyester, nylon, acetate, rayon, elastane, acrylic, metallic and many more, which are chemically produced.

A large variety of blends is available. Polyester/cotton has the comfort of cotton and the easy care of polyester. A wool and nylon blend will have the warmth of wool and the strength of nylon.

Fabrics are either woven, knitted or nonwoven. Plain weave construction is found in muslins, poplin and taffeta; denim and gaberdine are diagonal weaves; and cotton sateen is a satin weave. Jersey is a plain knit, and sweater knits can either be purl, patterned or raschel knit. Felt is a good example of a nonwoven fabric. Fabrics that are easy to handle are generally plain weave or firm knit, of medium weight.

Small prints, especially dark colours which hide stitching imperfections, are easy to sew and require no pattern matching.

Colour and texture

A single colour may appear to have certain qualities, but colour combinations can create a number of subtle optical illusions. Warm colours, for instance reds, oranges and yellows, appear to be more prominent than the cool colours such as blue, green and blue violet. The neutral colours – black and white – provide emphasis and contrast, intensifying each other, whereas greys and harmonious colours have a softening effect. Dark colours seem to reduce apparent figure size but light colours increase it. Any one colour in a print can be highlighted and used to accentuate specific features of a garment such as pockets, collars and cuffs.

Colour choice is very personal and you should always aim to enhance your features. Commercial schemes are available to help with assessing your colour characteristics. These schemes also recommend suitable colour combinations. It is, however, quite simple to develop your own style.

Dark colours appear to reduce size but light colours increase it

Warm reds appear more prominent than cool blues

Black and white are good contrasts

Greys and harmonious colours have a softening effect

Extract a colour from a print to accentuate collars and cuffs

The texture of fabric also plays an important role in appealing to the senses. Reflected light affects the colour of the fabric and also the apparent figure size. A dull finish will reduce size, whereas a shiny finish will appear to increase it.

The drape, which is the way fabric hangs on the body, is largely influenced by the suppleness or stiffness and the weight and body of the fabric. Bouclé or other rough textures are inclined to make the body look heavier. Petite people should be particularly aware of this.

A stiff fabric might well conceal the figure but will, at the same time, make it seem larger. However, the same silhouette in a soft, clinging fabric is figure-revealing. Fabrics with soft or crisp textures are a lot more flattering.

Wider spaces between vertical lines have an enlarging effect. This is more noticeable where the colours are contrasting than when muted shades are used. Textured effects can also be created by draping, ruching, quilting or stitching.

Testing fabrics

Instead of prewashing fabric, it is a better idea to take a swatch of fabric and conduct a few simple tests for shrinkage and colourfastness. Prewashing and dry cleaning are time consuming and expensive. Special finishes such as chintz may be damaged or washed away. However, washing and drying fabric prior to sewing is a matter of personal preference.

> Wool and wool blends need to be steamed and conditioned. Cotton and poly/cotton blends do benefit from the wash, dry and press steps. They often prevent the seams from puckering, which may happen the first time the garment is washed.

Smooth and rough textures

Stiff, firm fabrics as opposed to soft supple textures

The different effects from tonal and contrasting colours

Shrinkage test

1 Cut two pieces of fabric, each about 30 cm (12 in) square. Notch the warp or length which is parallel to the selvedge.

2 Place the iron (on high and full steam) on the first swatch for about 20 seconds, wait one minute, and repeat two or three times. Leave the swatch undisturbed for one hour. Thick wool and gaberdine need to condition for 4 hours as they tend to hold their moisture.

3 Measure both sides of the swatch after conditioning and compare these measurements to the original ones. The results will reveal whether any pre-steaming is necessary.

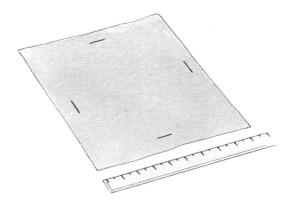

4 Wash the second swatch of fabric in warm water and leave for one hour to condition. Remeasure it and then compare these measurements to the original ones. This test will also expose any possible bleeding of the dye.

Depending on the desired fit of the garment, it is possible to bypass prewashing, especially when there is minimal shrinkage. About 2% in the length is commercially acceptable.

Seam slippage

This occurs when stress is placed on a seam. The yarns on either side separate and pull away from the stitching. A quick way to test for seam slippage is to hold a piece of fabric with the selvedge running vertically, place your thumb and middle finger of the same hand together on both sides of the fabric and pull. If the yarns do not recover, a fusible tape must be used to reinforce the seams.

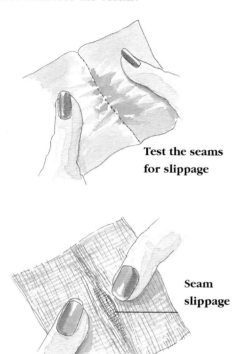

Test the seams for slippage

Seam slippage

Interfacings

Interfacing is one of the essential components of a successful, professionally finished garment. It gives the garment shape, support and stability. Be sure to select the correct quality of interfacing, taking the weight into account.

There are two types of interfacing, namely fusible and sew-in. Velvet, fake fur, synthetic leather, lace, mesh, vinyl, rainwear and plissé, as well as water-repellent and stain-resistant finishes are not suitable for the fusing process and sew-in interfacings need to be used here. Most other fabrics can be fused. The difference between the two types of interfacing is easily identifiable: the fusibles have a shiny resin or sugary appearance on the side that causes the bonding. Always remember to conduct a fuse test before applying your interfacings.

Fusing test

1 Cut a swatch of fabric and a piece of fusible interfacing half the size of the fabric swatch. Set the iron according to the manufacturer's specifications. Place the resin side of the interfacing on the wrong side of the fabric. Be sure not to stretch the interfacing.

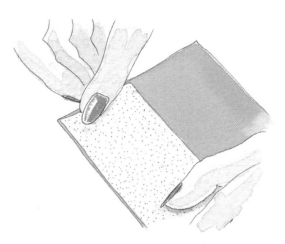

2 Cover the interfacing with a damp pressing cloth and place the iron on top, pressing firmly for the specified time. Should the iron not cover the entire swatch, pick up the iron and reposition it without sliding it along the fabric. Repeat as often as necessary. The fusing time is usually between 10 and 20 seconds.

3 Remove the pressing cloth, turn the swatch over and steam iron it. Leave for a while to settle or condition. Check whether the fabric has been bonded properly by trying to remove some of the fusing. At this stage you can also check whether the correct quality of fusible interfacing has been used for the desired effect.

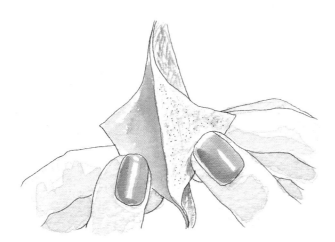

Advice from the professionals

- Be sure to use compatible interfacing and fabric, both of which require the same washing instructions.
- Use dark interfacings on dark fabrics and white or cream-coloured interfacings on light colours.
- Sandwich aluminium foil between the ironing board and its cover to act as a heat conductor.
- Pin the tricky areas where the interfacing may shift from the fabric.

Trouble spots

Bubbling
The interfacing has adhered unevenly to the fabric, causing a bubbling effect.

- Check your iron for even distribution of temperature. Lower the temperature slightly and fuse again, applying pressure. Alternatively, try another interfacing with a different bonding agent.

Delamination
The interfacing separates from the fabric after either steaming or washing.

- Check your iron for even distribution of temperature. Fuse again, applying pressure. Try another quality fusible.

Shrinkage
The fabric and interfacing are incompatible, causing either one to shrink.

- Lower the temperature of the iron and also reduce the fusing time. Do not steam when fusing and pressing.

Strike through
The bonding agent of the interfacing has seeped through the interfacing and may even stick onto the unfused fabric.

- Lower the temperature of the iron and also lessen the pressure. Use an interfacing with less bonding agent.

Blistering may be caused by the finish of the fabric, which in turn causes a breakdown of the bond between the interfacing and the fabric.

CUTTING PROCEDURE

Precision is essential when laying up and cutting out fabric. Small errors can multiply, altering the fit drastically. Grain lines also play an important role and can cause twisting or unwanted flaring when not taken into account. Inconsequential pattern pieces may be tilted slightly to prevent wastage when laying up, but refer to the chart below for the maximum tilt degrees. Please note that plaid and striped fabrics must be cut on their grain lines.

Tilting chart

Trouser front	1 degree
Trouser back	2 degrees
Trouser and skirt fly	1 degree
Trouser and skirt belt loops	1 degree
Pocket facing	2 degrees
Trouser and skirt front lining	1 degree
Trouser and skirt back lining	2 degrees
Waistcoat front lining	3 degrees
Waistcoat front facing	2 degrees

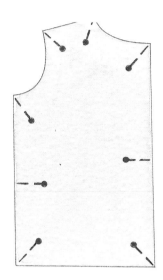

Designer tips

- Make sure the cutting surface is clean and smooth.
- Examine fabric for any flaws or imperfections.
- Snip selvedges that are too tight every so often.
- Double-check alterations to ensure that all corresponding seams match.
- Lay fabric right side up when pattern matching.

- Place pins perpendicular to the cutting lines and diagonally at the corners
- Lay out all pattern pieces before cutting.
- If tracing around a cardboard pattern piece onto the fabric, ensure that the chalk is sharpened.
- Thick lines can add extra measurement to each panel, resulting in a looser fit overall. Weigh down
- Be sure to cut left and right pieces when instructed to cut two.
- Check that the correct number of pieces are cut, especially pockets, welts and cuffs where you may need more than two pieces.

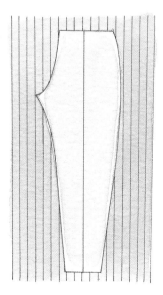

- Ensure that the gainline is perpendicular, especially with knits.

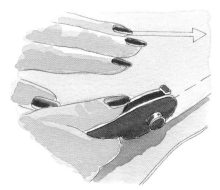

- Cut in one direction around the patterns so that the pattern pieces always fall away from the path of the blade

- Save fabric scraps for testing tension, interfacings and pressing, as well as for making covered buttons or bound buttonholes.

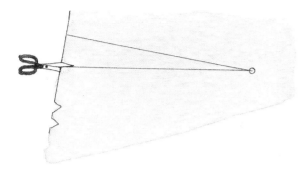

- Use the point of the scissors to cut notches. Do this on completion of each piece.

- Mark lace with coloured chalk instead of snipping.

Hints on notching

Notches are mainly used to indicate key match points for seams. It is easier to snip into the seam allowance than to cut out the V. However, some knits and lace may be difficult to snip and should be marked with coloured chalk. Centre front and backs should also be notched, as well as any other fold lines. To eliminate tailor's tacks, the start of darts and tucks may also be notched.

Commercially, holes are drilled into the fabric to indicate dart points and pocket positioning. This can weaken the fabric if done domestically, and is therefore not advised. Mark these points with a marker, pins or tailor's tacks as illustrated on page 44.

Bias binding

Because the bias of the fabric is more elastic than the warp, bias-cut strips are often used to bind curved edges such as necklines and armholes. To find the true bias, simply fold the fabric diagonally so that the warp and the weft meet, as illustrated. Cut along the fold line and mark further strips parallel to this line, using chalk or a soft marker. Join the strips as required.

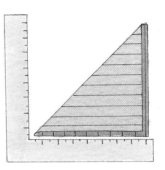

Fold fabric diagonally

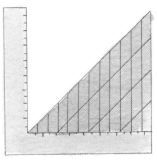

Mark and cut strips

Join strips in this direction

If bias binding is required, try to mark it between the pattern pieces when laying them out on the fabric. This will eliminate fabric wastage. The strips may also be cut slightly off the true bias if necessary.

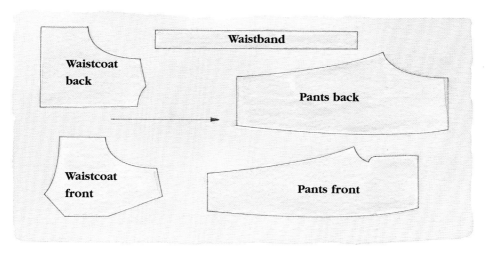

Example of laying out velvet

Directional fabrics

Fabrics with nap, pile, sheen or one-way designs need to be cut in the same direction. Napped fabric, such as fleece, is brushed after weaving. The yarns of velvet and corduroy are cut to result in a furry pile. Cutting fabric with the nap, pile or smooth side down will give a lighter, shinier look, whereas nap running up will result in a richer, deeper colour. The fabric will feel rough when stroked downwards. Satins and brocades need to be cut in the same direction to eliminate shading. The designs on printed fabric need to be examined to avoid something ending upside down!

Pattern matching

Plaids, stripes and large prints need to be aligned when cut. A simple way of doing this is first to lay up and cut out the one side of the garment, and then place the cut pieces face side down on the fabric, matching any patterns, as illustrated. This way, stripes and plaids can be perfectly matched even when cut on the bias.

Alternative method of pattern matching

Lay out the fabric face side up. Fold in half lengthwise, matching the pattern at the selvedges. If no pattern pieces need to be cut on the fold, cut the fabric along the fold, i.e. lengthwise. This makes the next step much easier. Holding the corners of the top layer, slowly roll the fabric back in the length, checking that the pattern is aligned with the bottom layer. If not, realign the layers until they match. Repeat this procedure across the width, rolling back from the selvedge. Realign as required and lay out the pattern pieces matching the key points, as illustrated.

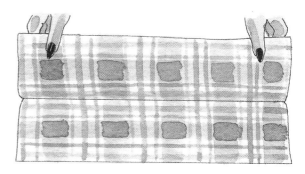

Key match points

These match points are places along the seams where checks, stripes and patterns must be lined up. Most are identified with notches.

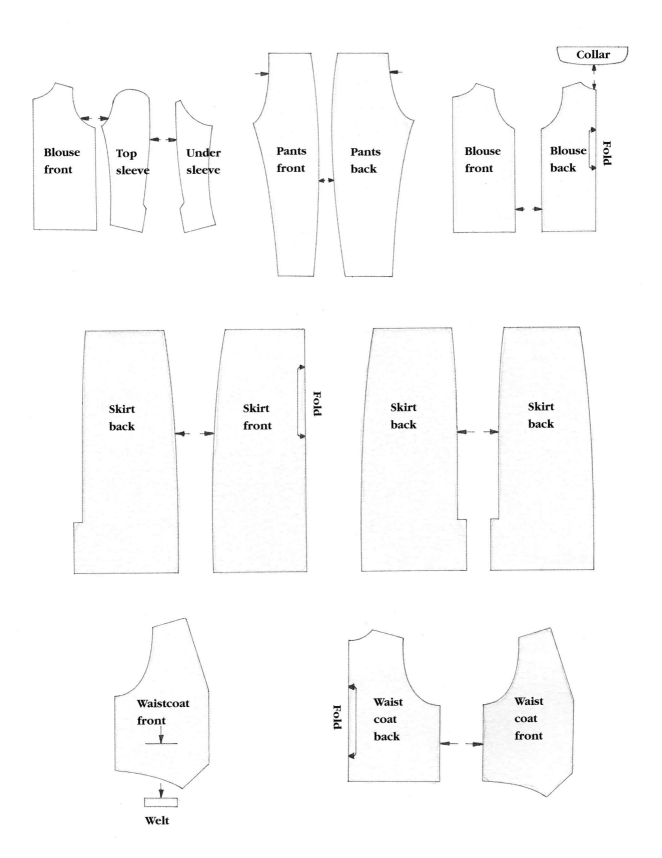

TECHNIQUES

The secret of a professionally made garment is executing the necessary techniques with the utmost accuracy and care. Nothing can make a garment look worse than mismatched darts, uneven gathering or badly stitched corners. These finer details, as well as accurate buttonholes, appropriate buttons and suitable zips, all assist in producing a chic garment. Thierry Mugler's attention to detail is clearly visible in this cerise dress. The stitching of all hems should also be done with care and precision, as they can so easily make a garment look home-made. The key to ultimate success is to press the garment after stitching each operation.

STITCHES

There are some sewing techniques which are best done by hand; others are more suited to machine stitching. When threading a needle, cut the thread at an angle using sharp scissors. Hand-sew with a shortish thread to avoid unnecessary knotting, and use a single thread except when attaching buttons and other fasteners. Select a needle that is suitable for the thread and the fabric. Polyester thread will not leave an impression after pressing. Silk twist is used for buttons, buttonholes and decorative sewing. Allow the thread to untwist itself by letting it dangle down and then sliding your fingers gently down the thread.

Basic handstitches

BACKSTITCH

This is the strongest hand stitch and is used for repairs to seams and in hard-to-reach areas where machine stitching is difficult. It resembles machine stitching on the right side and overlapping stitches on the underside.

Bring the needle and thread to the upper side of the work. Insert the needle through all the layers of fabric behind the point where the thread emerges, bringing the needle out the same distance in front of that point. Continue inserting and bringing up the needle and thread half a stitch length behind and in front of the previous stitch.

BLINDSTITCH

This stitch is worked between the hem and the garment so that the stitches are not visible. It also prevents the top of the hem from making a ridge on the right side of the garment.

Work from the right to the left with the needle pointing left. Roll the hem edge back about 6 mm (¼ in), taking a very small horizontal stitch in the garment. Take the next stitch about 6 mm (¼ in) in the hem, to the left of the first stitch. Continue to alternate these stitches about 6 mm (¼ in) apart. Ensure that stitches on the garment side remain small and do not pull up tightly.

'One shouldn't spend all one's time dressing. All one needs are two or three suits, as long as they, and everything to go with them, are perfect.'

Coco Chanel

HERRINGBONE

This is a strong hemming stitch which is mainly used on pinked edges. The thread crosses over itself forming a zigzag pattern. It may also be worked between the hem and the garment as for blindstitching, and is particularly suitable for heavy fabrics because of its stable and secure results.

Work from the left to the right with the needle pointing left. Fasten the thread on the wrong side of the hem and insert the needle through the hem edge. Take a very small horizontal stitch in the garment directly above the hem edge and about 6 mm (¼ in) to 1 cm (⅜ in) to the right. Take the next stitch about 6 mm (¼ in) to 1 cm (⅜ in) to the right in the hem. Continue to alternate these stitches, spacing them evenly. Ensure that the stitches remain small and do not pull up tightly.

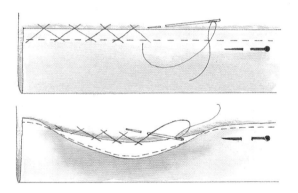

FRENCH TACKS

These are used to link two separate garment sections together, such as a loose lining to a hem.

Take a small stitch in the seam of the hem and then another through the lining directly opposite, allowing about 2 cm (¾ in) to 5 cm (2 in) slack between these two stitches. Repeat a few times and then work closely spaced blanket stitches over these

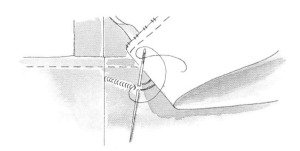

threads by keeping the thread from the previous stitch under the point of the needle and then drawing the needle and thread through to form a stitch over the edge.

PRICKSTITCH

This stitch is a variation of backstitch. On the right side the stitches are very short with long spaces between them. It is mainly used to insert a zip by hand or for decorative topstitching.

Bring the needle and thread through the fabric to the upper side. Insert the needle through the fabric, one or two fabric threads behind the point where the needle came out. Bring the needle up 3 mm (⅛ in) to 6 mm (¼ in) in front of the point where the thread emerged. The top surface stitches should be very small pricks.

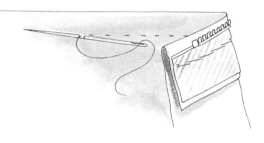

RUNNING STITCH

This stitch is used for hand basting. It temporarily holds two or more layers of fabric together for fitting or stitching. It is a short, even stitch which is also suitable for tucking, gathering and even mending.

Work from the right to the left, weaving the point of the needle in and out of the fabric a few times before pulling the thread through. These short, even stitches should be about 6 mm (¼ in) long.

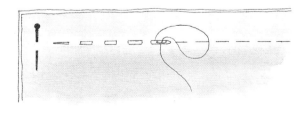

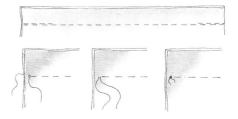
SLIPSTITCH

This is an almost invisible stitch which is formed by slipping the thread under a fold of fabric. It is used to hem, tack and finish facings, as well as to join two folded edges together, or to join one folded edge to a flat surface.

Work from the right to the left, holding the folded edge in your left hand. Bring the needle up through the fold, taking a stitch into the garment directly opposite the point where the thread comes out and only catching one or two threads. Slip the needle through the fold about 6 mm (¼ in) further and continue taking stitches about 6 mm (¼ in) apart. When joining two folded edges, make the stitches on both sides the same size, as illustrated.

TACKING

This stitch is used for holding two pieces of fabric together temporarily. It is much like running stitch, except that the stitches are longer and further apart.

Follow the same instructions as for running stitch.

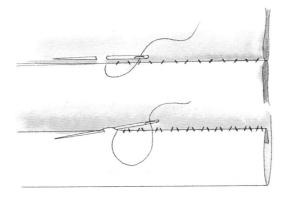

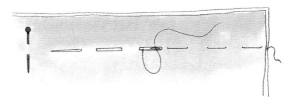

Although there are numerous other hand stitches, these are the most popular.

Basic machine stitches

STAYSTICHING

This is a line of regular stitching which is done slightly closer to the edge of the fabric than the actual seam. It is used on curves and angles such as necklines and waistlines to prevent them from stretching while handling. Preferably stitch in line with the grain.

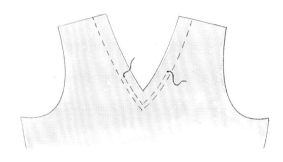

REINFORCING

This extra stitching is done on the seam line to strengthen the fabric at points of strain. It is also used at corners or curves that need clipping, such as a V-neck or a square neck.

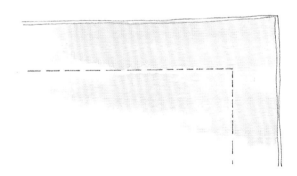

UNDERSTITCHING

This straight stitching is used to keep the facings from rolling to the right side of the garment. Trim, clip and press the seam allowance towards the facing and then stitch on the right side of the facing, close to the seam line.

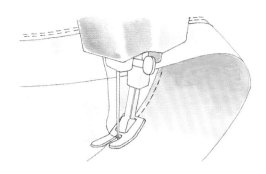

TOPSTITCHING

This decorative stitch is done on the right side of the garment, using either all-purpose thread or topstitching thread. It can either be stitched close to the edge, about 6 mm (¼ in) to 1 cm (⅜ in) from the edge, or combined for a twin-needled effect. Lengthen the stitch slightly and loosen the tension for a more pronounced look.

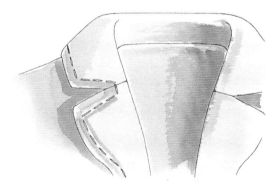

EASING

This row of stitching is done on the seam line of a single layer of fabric when slight fullness is required on one side and no fullness on the corresponding side. Lengthen the stitches and loosen the tension, then pull up slightly but evenly to fit the other edge.

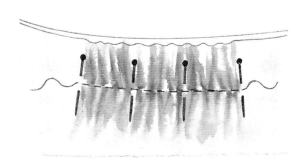

SEAM FINISHES

The finish of a seam will lend a couture touch and improved appearance to a garment. Seams need to be finished to prevent wovens from fraying and knits from curling. They also strengthen the seams and help to maintain a new appearance. Finish a seam as it is stitched, before it is crossed by another. Experiment with scrap fabric before deciding on a specific finish.

Basic seam finishes

SELVEDGE

If the garment is cut using the selvedge as the edge, diagonal snips must be made on this selvedge to prevent shrinking and puckering. Snip at about 7.5 cm (3 in) to 10 cm (4 in) intervals after the seam has been stitched.

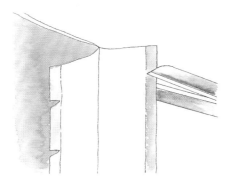

STITCHED AND PINKED

This finish is suitable for firmly-woven fabric. Stitch 6 mm (¼ in) from the edge of each seam allowance. Press seam open and trim the excess close to the stitching with pinking shears.

TURNED AND STITCHED

Use this method for lightweight fabrics only. Stitch 3 mm (⅛ in) to 6 mm (¼ in) from the edge of each seam allowance. This stitching is optional, but helps the edge turn under, especially on curves. Turn the edge under on the stitching line and stitch close to the edge of the fold, but only through the seam allowance. Press the seam open.

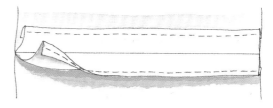

ZIGZAG

This finish is particularly good for knits because it has more give than straight stitching. Either zigzag close to the edge and trim off the excess, being careful not to cut any stitches, or stitch so that the stitches go over the edge. If the fabric puckers, loosen the tension.

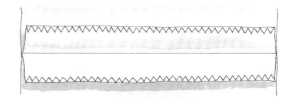

Overlocked

This stitch requires an overlocker machine which will edge and trim off the raw edges simultaneously. This method is quick and effective and is becoming more and more popular amongst dressmakers.

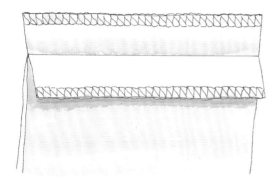

Bias-bound seams

Bias binding is used to enclose the raw edges of the seams. This enhances the inside finish of the garment and is a good choice for unlined jackets. Edgestitch the binding onto the seam edge.

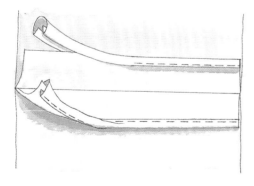

Bound seams (Hong Kong finish)

This is a technique used by couturiers to enclose the raw edges. Cut bias strips of lining about 32 mm (1¼ in) wide. Align the bias strips on the right side of the seam allowance and stitch 6 mm (¼ in) from the cut edge. Trim the seam allowance of any heavy fabric. Press the bias strip back over the cut edge of the seam allowance; fold the bias strip to the underside, enclosing the cut edge. Pin the bias strip in place and stitch in the ditch or groove between the bias and the fabric. This stitching will be hidden on the right side and will catch the bias on the underside. Press lightly.

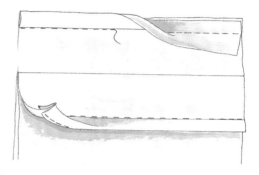

Flat-fell seam

This seam is popular in menswear, children's play clothes, denim jeans and reversible garments. It is a sturdy seam where both raw edges are enclosed. Stitch with wrong sides together, taking 1.5 cm (⅝ in) seam allowance. Press the seam allowances to one side and trim the lower seam allowance to 3 mm (⅛ in). Turn under 6 mm (¼ in) on the upper seam allowance and press. Pin the folded seam allowance to the garment, concealing the trimmed lower edge. Edgestitch on the fold, removing the pins as you stitch. The finished seam is reversible.

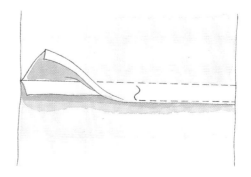

Welt or Mock flat-fell seam

This seam is also called a double-stitched welt seam. It is easier to sew than the real thing, and has the same appearance. However, one raw edge is exposed and might require overlocking. With right sides facing, stitch a plain seam and press the seam allowances to the one side. Trim the lower seam allowance to 6 mm (¼ in). Topstitch on the right side of the garment 6 mm (¼ in) to 12 mm (½ in) from the seam line. This finished seam is called a welt seam. For the mock flat-felled seam, edgestitch close to the seam line. The twin-needled seam will resemble a flat-fell seam on the right side, but has one exposed seam allowance on the wrong side.

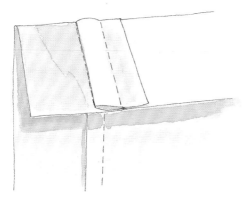

Welt seam

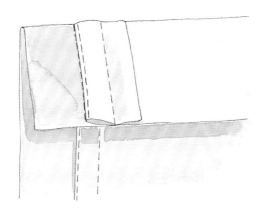

Mock flat-felled seam

French seam

This seam is suitable for sheer and other lightweight fabrics. It is often used on blouses, unlined jackets, lingerie and children's clothes. With the wrong sides facing, stitch about 1 cm (⅜ in) from the edge. Trim the seam allowances back to 3 mm (⅛ in). Fold the right sides together so that the stitching line is exactly on the fold. Stitch 6 mm (¼ in) from the fold, encasing the cut edges. Press the seam allowance to one side. This seam is best used on straight seams as it is difficult to sew on the curve.

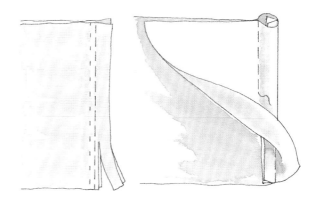

Mock French seam

This seam can be used on curved or straight seams. With right sides facing, stitch a plain seam, trim the seam allowances to 12 mm (½ in) and press open. On each seam allowance, press 6 mm (¼ in) towards the inside of the seam. Stitch the edges close to the folds, as illustrated. Press the seam to one side.

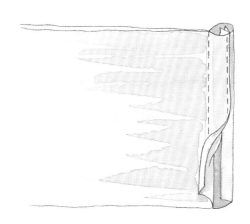

CORNERS

Corners are located mainly on collars, cuffs and pockets. These focal points need to be well constructed in order to achieve a professional-looking garment. A sharp turn in the stitching line is not essential. Blunting the corner is the best way to achieve a precise point on an enclosed seam. Mitring hems and pocket corners is another alternative. A simple facing can also finish off a corner.

ENCLOSED CORNER

Sew one stitch diagonally across the corner of a fine fabric, two stitches on a medium weight and three stitches on bulky fabric, as illustrated. Trim the seam allowance across the corner and then taper on either side. To set the stitches, first press them flat, then press the seams open, preferably using a point presser. Turn to the right side and, using an awl or the point of the scissors, carefully coax out the corner. Press again.

A quick alternative is to use the finger pressing technique, especially for collars and waistbands. Having stitched and trimmed the corner, fold the seam allowance and turn the work right side out using your fingers.

INWARD CORNER

First reinforce the inward corner, stitching just inside the seam line for approximately 2 cm (¾ in) on either side. Snip right up into this corner, being careful not to cut into the stitches. The inward corner can now be joined with an outward corner or straight edge, as illustrated.

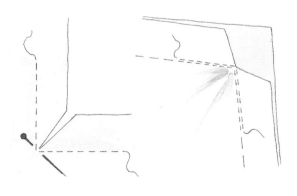

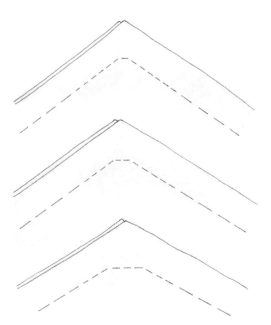

Mitred hem

Fold back both seam lines and press. Open out the edges and fold back the corner, aligning the crease lines. Press. Open out the corner and fold the garment diagonally with right sides facing and raw edges together. Stitch along the diagonal press line, as illustrated. Trim the seam allowance to 6 mm (¼ in) and taper the corner. Press the seam open, turn right side out and press again.

Mitred straight trim

Attach the trim to the garment by stitching along the outer edge of the trim. Stop at the corner and back stitch. Fold the trim back on itself so that the edges align with the garment, as illustrated. Pin in place. Press the diagonal fold formed at the corner. Lift up the trim, stitch along the diagonal line and trim the seam to 6 mm (¼ in). Fold the trim back into position and stitch from the corner, starting in the last stitch, along the outer edge of the trim. The inner edge can now be stitched. Press the complete trim and garment.

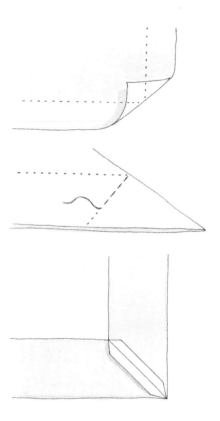

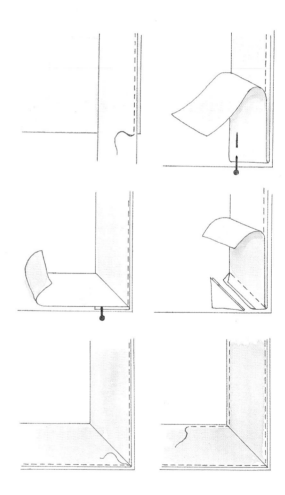

The Chanel jacket, a particular style of jacket made known by the revered Parisian couturier, Coco Chanel, incorporates the use of mitring techniques. The famous Japanese designer, Issey Miyake, hems all the edges of his unlined creations and where two of these edges meet, he usually mitres the corners.

TRIMMING

For smooth, professional-looking seams, it might be necessary to trim some of the seam allowance away. The amount that is trimmed off will depend on whether the fabric frays or not. The type of seam stitched, for instance French seams, will also indicate whether the seam requires trimming or not. To avoid making a ridge, the seams can be graded, as illustrated. This is especially important when there are a few layers of fabric or when the fabric is bulky. Trimming corners, as previously discussed, is also essential.

Curved seams need to be notched and clipped to allow them to lie smoothly. Convex or outward curves have to be snipped or clipped to enable the edges to spread. Using sharp scissors, snip, just short of the seam line, at various intervals. Concave or inward curves have to be notched. Wedges are cut from the seam allowance enabling the edges to draw in. Use sharp scissors to notch at various intervals.

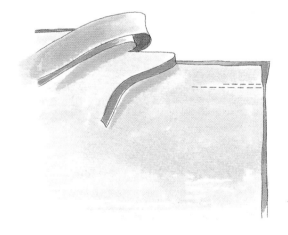

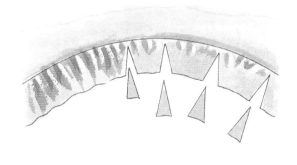

In a princess seam, where the clips and notches face one another, they should be staggered to avoid weakening the fabric. Staystitching the concave seam before notching it will also strengthen the seam.

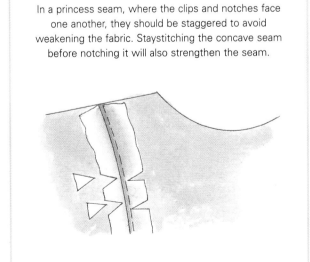

PRESSING

Pressing means lifting the iron and setting it down again in the required position. It sets stitches, flattens seams and edges, creases the folds and shapes the garment. To accomplish the well-defined edges and sculptured contours of a couture garment, it is essential to press as you sew. Pressing is an integral part of the assembly process and should not be ignored simply to hasten the task. All the necessary equipment for pressing should be set up near your sewing machine for convenience.

Fabrics need to be tested for their reaction to heat, moisture and pressure. Use the temperature setting on the iron as a guide when testing. Moisture comes from the steam emitted from the sole plate, the spray released from the front of the iron or from a damp cloth. To avoid water marks, shield the fabric with a pressing cloth. Gabardine, for instance, should not be steamed but requires moisture along with a pressing cloth to crease the edges and flatten the seams. Lightweight irons may be adequate for ironing wrinkles but thick fabrics need the pressure of a heavier iron. Pressure needs to be applied manually when the iron isn't heavy enough, but this must be carefully gauged as too much pressure can so easily give the fabric an old, worn appearance.

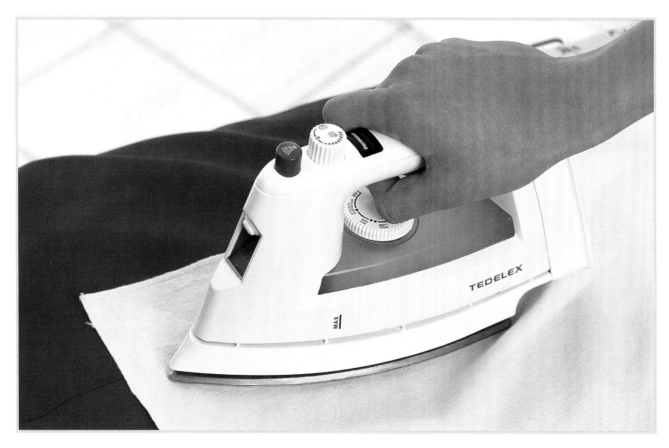

Use a pressing cloth to protect the fabric

Pressing tips

- Iron fabric before cutting, sliding the iron with the grain of the fabric.
- Be sure not to stretch the edges and curves by pulling the fabric.
- Press on the inside as you sew.
- Press in the direction you have stitched and do not press over pins.
- Always press seams and darts before they are crossed with other seams.
- Preferably press on the wrong side of the fabric, alternatively, use a pressing cloth.
- Use brown paper strips to prevent impressions of seam allowances, darts or pleats (*see* below).
- Snip or notch curved seams before pressing.
- Press seams at finished edges where allowances are completely enclosed, such as collars, cuffs and pocket flaps, before turning out.

- Cotton and linen are best pressed when damp. After pressing, allow all fabric to cool and dry.
- Press embroidery and lace face down on a padded surface like towelling. Velvet and corduroy should be pressed on a needle board (*see* below).

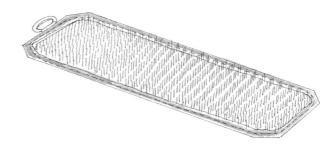

A technique often used by the couturiers instead of pressing a hem, especially where a soft hem is required, is to steam the hem and then pat lightly to mould it.

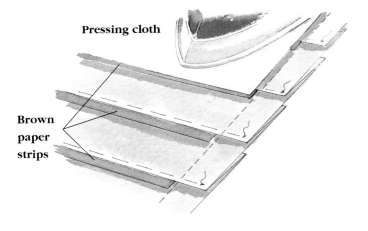

Pressing cloth

Brown paper strips

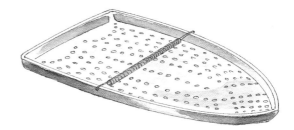

- Use a Teflon sleeve (*see* above) on the sole plate of the iron to avoid 'shining' the fabric.
- Press the seam allowance with the tip of the iron, for instance to shrink some of the fullness on a sleeve head.
- Above all, do not overpress.

DARTS

Darts are used to build a curved shape into a flat piece of fabric. They are one of the most basic structural elements in dressmaking and occur most often at the bust, front and back waist and hip, and also less frequently at the back shoulder and elbow. Because they need to be positioned and stitched accurately, precision is essential. Marking methods may vary according to preference.

Marking

There are various techniques for transferring the pattern markings to the fabric. Because of the different weights, types and textures of fabrics, it is necessary to choose the method best suited to the fabric used.

Tailor's tacks

This is the best method for marking delicate fabric because the tacks are easy to remove and do not cause permanent damage to the fabric. Use cotton tacking thread, a fine silk thread or two strands of embroidery thread.

1 At each dart point or interior dart marking, make a small single stitch through both layers of fabric and the tissue pattern pieces. Leave a 5 cm (2 in) unknotted thread tail on each side of the stitch.

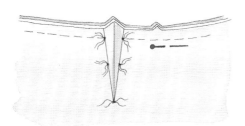

2 Carefully lift the pattern off the fabric, raise the top layer of fabric about 2.5 cm (1 in) and cut the threads between the two fabric layers.

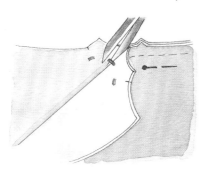

Dressmaker's tracing paper and wheel

Using this method, a single mark or an entire line can be simultaneously transferred onto two layers of (preferably opaque) fabric. This technique is especially helpful when marking an uneven dart under a notched collar.

1 Start with a piece of tracing paper, tracing side up, then place both fabric pattern pieces, right sides facing, on top of the tracing paper. Place a second piece of tracing paper, tracing side down, on top of the fabric. Finally place the tissue pattern piece on top of the second piece of tracing paper. Trace the dart on the tissue pattern using the wheel.

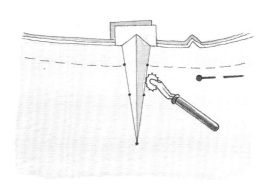

2 Top the dart point with a short line perpendicular to the centre of the dart and trace other interior dart markings similarly.

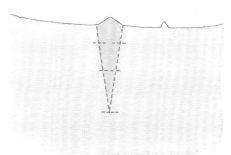

Chalk and wax

This is the most efficient way of marking a dart formed with pins. A series of marks or even a single mark is made where the pins are placed.

1 Insert the pins through the marks on the tissue pattern and both layers of the fabric. Turn the pattern and the fabric pieces over, push each pin in the direction of the dart point and then rub the chalk pencil or wax on the fabric over each pin, leaving short lines.

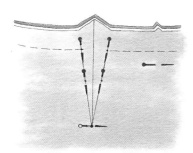

2 Turn the fabric and pattern pieces over again and carefully pull the pattern off, holding each pin in place from the bottom. Angling the pins in the direction of the dart sides, rub the chalk pencil or wax on the fabric over each pin.

Contouring

When patternmaking, straight lines are used to make dart sides. However, these lines create a point and should be slightly shortened and contoured. For instance, the point of the bust dart should end 2.5 cm (1 in) to 5 cm (2 in) away from the bust point. Constructing darts to follow the body's contours will give the best fit.

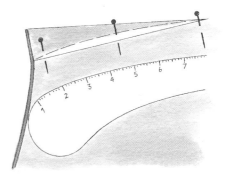

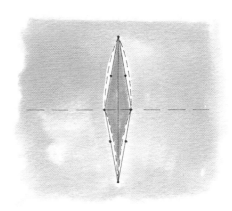

If wrinkles form below the waist on trousers and skirts, remove the excess fabric by widening the back darts. If, for instance, the darts are straining over a high hip area, release some of the dart by contouring. Lower the top of the dart for a low bust. Narrow the dart intake for a thick waist.

Stitching

With right sides together, fold the dart in half, matching the dart points and notches. At this point the dart can be chalked in, contoured as desired and then stitched. Stitch from the wide end of the dart, using backstitching as reinforcement, to the point, securing the point by knotting the threads. Be sure to taper the last few stitches very close to the fold. Fisheye or contoured darts should be stitched from the widest part tapering to the one point; then turn the garment around to complete the balance of the dart in the same manner.

Backstitching often results in puckering because the previous line of stitching was not duplicated exactly, hence knotting at the point is advised. Another method to follow is to advance to the point, pivot the work and sew a few stitches back into the dart.

Pressing

After the dart has been stitched, it is essential to press the dart correctly before the major seams are stitched. Keeping the dart folded as for stitching, press towards the point, being careful not to press beyond it, thus creasing the rest of the garment. Spread open the garment over the curved surface of a press mitt to maintain the shape, and then press.

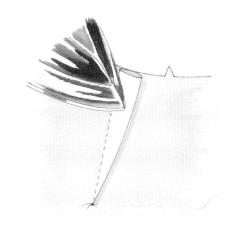

Vertical darts should be pressed towards the centre front or centre back and horizontal darts are pressed downwards. Deep darts must be trimmed and pressed open with the point pressed flat. Curved darts should be slashed or clipped to relieve any strain.

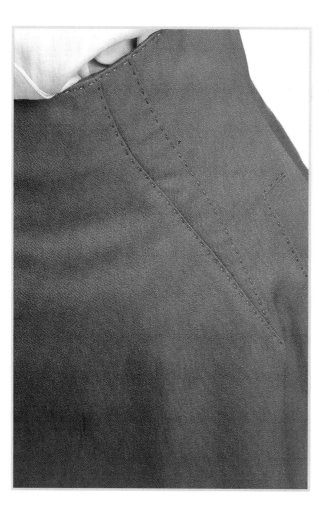

LEFT: Darts can be topstitched to accentuate the shaping.

TUCKS

Tucks are folds of fabric stitched down either all or part of the way, such as released tucks. Their purpose is mainly decorative although they may also be used as a shaping device. They are usually folded on the straight and each tuck is formed from two stitching lines that are matched and stitched. The distance from the fold to the matching line determines the tuck's width. Tucks that meet or overlap slightly are called blind tucks; those with predetermined space between them are spaced tucks; and a pintuck is a very narrow tuck, usually about 3 mm (⅛ in) wide. Light to medium weight fabrics are suitable for tucking, but design and print should be considered before purchasing the fabric. Tucks can be added to plain garments by pretucking the fabric before it is cut.

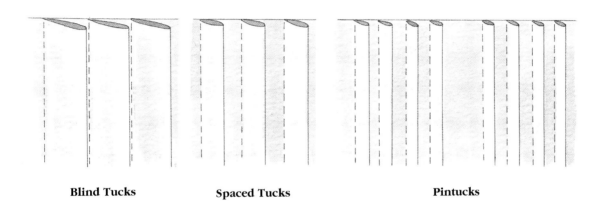

Blind Tucks   **Spaced Tucks**   **Pintucks**

Notch the stitching lines for the tucks at the start and finish of each tuck. Establish the spacing between each tuck and use a cardboard gauge to maintain an even width when stitching. Stitch the tucks in the order illustrated. Begin with the centre tuck, stitching downwards; next the tucks on either side, stitching upwards; then the tucks on either side of those, stitching downwards, and so on. This will keep the tucks straight and prevent puckering. Press each tuck individually, using a pressing cloth, before pressing all the tucks in the direction required.

Fancy tucks

SHELL TUCKS
First stitch the tuck, then handstitch a few overhand stitches every 1 cm (⅜ in) to form a scallop. Alternatively, blindstitch by machine, with the tuck under the foot and the fold to the left of the needle, allowing the zigzag stitch to scallop the tuck.

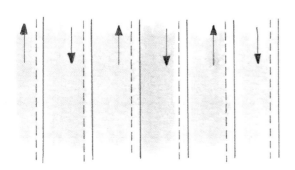

CORDED TUCKS

Fold the tuck, positioning the cord inside the tuck along the fold. Pin in position and, using a zip foot, stitch close to the cord.

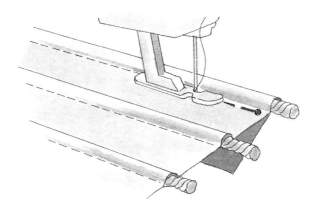

CROSS TUCKS

First stitch the lengthwise tucks and press in one direction, then form the cross tucks at right angles to the first set and stitch. Be sure to keep the first set of tucks facing downwards.

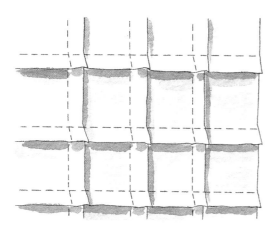

RELEASED TUCKS

These dart tucks are usually used to control fullness at the bust or hip. They are mainly formed inside and can be released at one or both ends. Be sure to reinforce the ends. Press carefully to avoid creasing the folds.

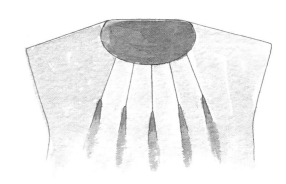

UNPRESSED PLEATS

These tucks are similar to the released tucks but are not darted in shape. The fabric is tucked to fit a specific measurement, but these tucks are usually not stitched down. Their depth may be as desired.

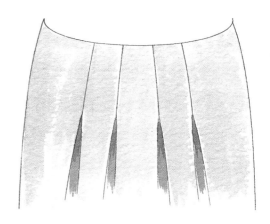

Calculating fabric quantities

Establish the depth and the number of tucks required. Double the depth and multiply by the number of tucks. This amount must then be added to the finished width of the pattern piece.

PLEATS

Pleats are folds of fabric that are pressed flat along the fold lines. They provide controlled fullness and may occur as a single pleat, as a cluster or around the entire garment. In vertical pleats, the fold line should always be on the straight grain, at least from the hip down. This ensures that the pleat hangs correctly. Fabric choice should be carefully considered. A smooth, crisp, light to medium weight fabric, such as gabardine, will pleat easily, as will fabrics containing polyester. Other synthetics, such as acrylic, will resist creasing and make pleating difficult, but not impossible.

Dry-cleaning a pleated garment is preferable as the garment will automatically be re-pressed whereas domestic laundering will necessitate re-forming and pressing the pleats with each wash. Edgestitching will facilitate this.

Knife pleats positioned on the left hand side only

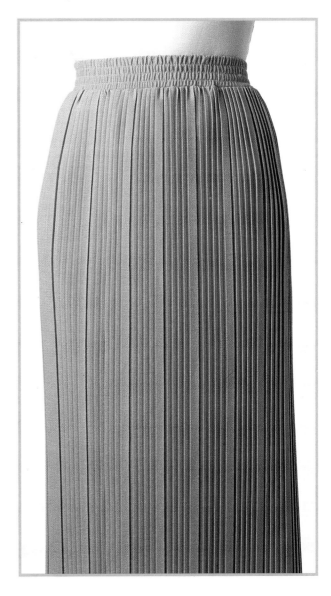

Commercially pleated fancy knife pleats

There are four basic pleats: knife pleats, which all face one way; box pleats, which have two folds turned away from one another; inverted pleats, which have two folds turned towards each other and meeting; and accordion pleats, which are narrow and have a zigzag appearance resembling the bellows of an accordion. These should be done by a commercial pleater, whereas the others can be done manually. For a more permanent finish, however, all pleats are best done by the professional pleaters, because they have the facilities to heat set the fabric.

Accordion Pleats

The inverted pleat can also be done with a separate underlay. This method is usually applicable when only a few pleats are required, but is not practicable for continuous pleating.

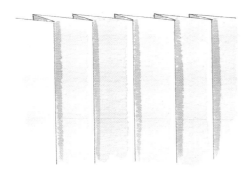

Knife Pleats

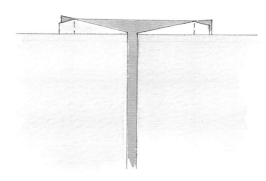

Inverted Pleat with Separate Underlay

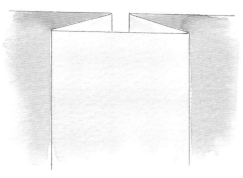

Box Pleat

Another pleat which can only be done by commercial pleaters is the sunray pleat. This one resembles the accordion pleat, but fans out like the rays of the sun and therefore has to be cut in a half circle, as illustrated.

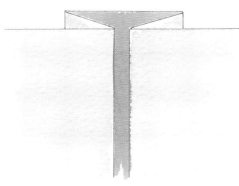

Inverted Pleat

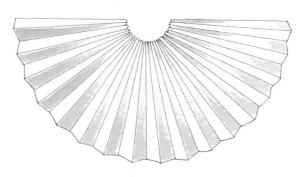

Sunray Pleats

Forming pleats

Pleats are formed by aligning the fold line with the placement line. The underlay, which is the space between these two lines, may be shallow or deep, depending on the choice of fabric and the fullness required. When planning a pleated garment, ensure that the hip measurement, with added ease, is applied. Each pleat can then be adjusted to attain the waist measurement, as illustrated. In this way, the pleats will fall closed. Topstitching will also keep the pleats in position.

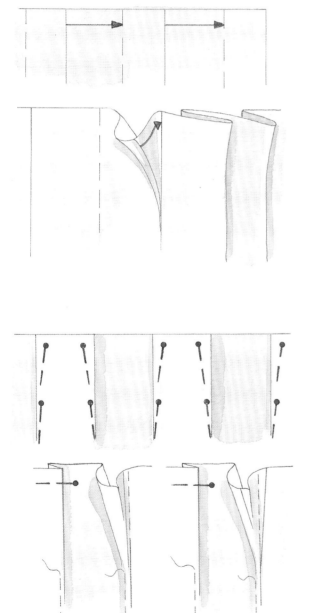

Sewing pleats

1 Join the side seams and hem the fabric before pleating it. Press well.

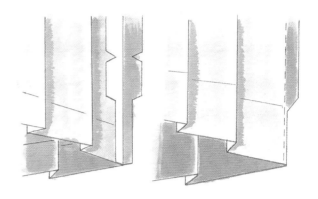

2 Notch the pleats at one end and pin the corresponding positions at the hem. Mark the fold lines and the placement lines accordingly.

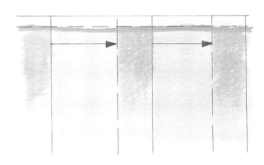

3 Pleat up the fabric matching these lines and then pin in position.

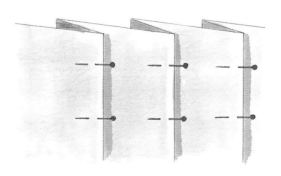

4 Hand or machine tack the pleats along the fold lines. Remove the pins.

5 Press the pleats lightly in the direction they will face.

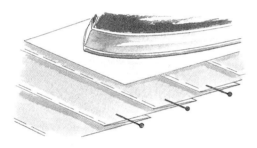

6 After pressing them, machine tack the pleats across the upper edge.

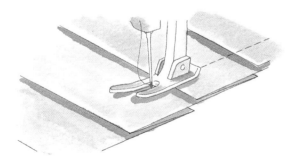

For pleats with separate underlays, first hem each panel and then join the seams. This will hold the pleat firmly in position. Trim the corners of the seam allowances at the hem diagonally and then whipstitch the edges, as illustrated on page 85.

7 With wrong side up, place strips of brown paper under each pleat to prevent an imprint of the pleat on the right side. Press again to set the pleats. Turn to the right side and steam pleats using a pressing cloth. Leave to dry on the ironing board.

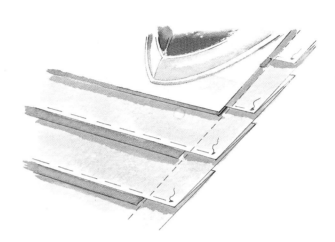

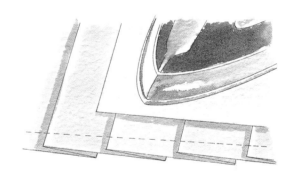

8 Topstitch the pleats if required and remove all the tacking threads.

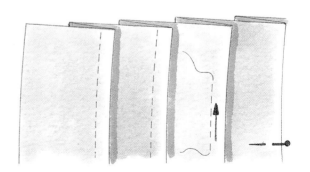

GATHERING

Gathers are formed when drawing up a specific amount of fabric to fit into a smaller area. This fullness adds a soft, feminine touch to a garment and can be found mostly at waistlines, cuffs, yokes, necklines or at sleeve heads. Gathering soft fabrics will have a draped effect, whereas crisp fabrics will billow out. In gathering, the bobbin thread is pulled up and a looser upper tension facilitates the sliding of the fabric along the thread.

1 Lengthen the stitch setting and loosen the upper tension on the machine appropriate to the fabric. Stitch the first row just above the seam line on the right side of the fabric and the second row 6 mm (¼ in) higher, leaving long threads.

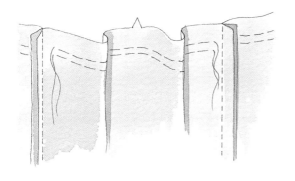

> Break the stitching at seams as it is difficult to gather through two thicknesses.

2 Pin the stitched edge to the corresponding straight edge on the garment, with right sides facing, matching any appropriate notches and seams.

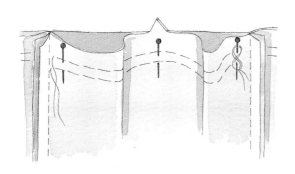

3 Carefully pull up the bobbin threads on the one side, sliding the fabric along. When half the gathered fabric fits the straight edge, secure the thread by twisting a figure eight around the pin. Repeat the process from the other side.

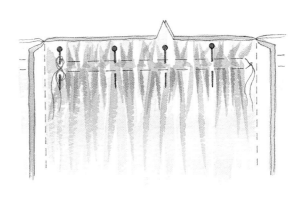

4 Adjust the gathers uniformly along the straight edge and pin them down, perpendicular to the stitching, and at frequent intervals.

5 Reset the stitch length and the tension on the machine. With the gathered side up, stitch on the seam line, holding the fabric on either side to avoid stitching little pleats.

6 Trim corners of the seams diagonally and press the seam allowance with the tip of the iron.

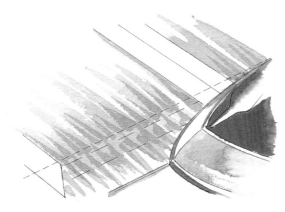

7 Overlock or zigzag the seam edge, open out the garment and then press the seam in the direction it will lie when finished. (Usually, it will point away from the gathers.)

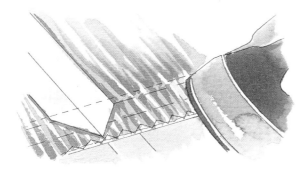

8 Press the gathers, sliding the point of the iron up into the gathers. Do not press across the gathers, as they will flatten and become limp.

Easing

Easing is not as full as gathering. It reduces the length of an area that needs to fit into a shorter area. Invariably, there is excess fullness or perhaps a dart that needs to be spread over a specific area. Most sleeve heads require a certain amount of easing to fit the curved shape into the almost straight section of the armhole. The differential feed on an industrial machine can be set to ease a given amount to a specific measurement. It can be done manually, either by pinning at frequent intervals or by following the instructions for gathering.

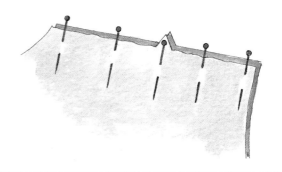

When easing, use an awl to position the excess fabric by gently pushing more fabric under the presser foot.

RIGHT: This smocked dress has gathers at the waist and on the sleeves to add the necessary fullness required.

Shirring

Shirring is formed by a number of rows of gathering. This method of controlling fullness is quite often enhanced with smocking. Shirring can also be elasticized to hug the body neatly. Elastic thread is used in the bobbin and regular thread in the needle. Lightweight fabrics such as voiles, batistes, crepes and jerseys are most suited to shirring. Ensure that the rows are straight, parallel and equidistant. Gather up the rows of stitching as for gathering, tying up the ends carefully, as illustrated.

Gathering with elastic

Elastic can be threaded through a casing, as illustrated, to gather up a waistline or form a frilled cuff. Tape or binding can be used for the casing. Elastic can also be stitched directly onto the garment, as illustrated. Pin the required length of elastic at either end of the seam line and pin the centre of the elastic to the centre of the fabric. Repeat at frequent intervals. With elastic side up, stitch elastic to fabric, stretching the elastic between the pins, with one hand behind the needle and the other hand at the following pin. Two rows of straight stitching or zigzag stitching may be used.

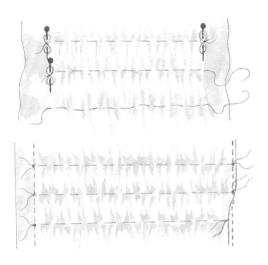

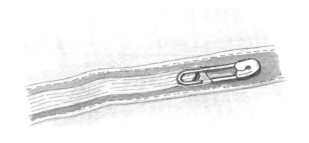

For elasticized shirring, wind the elastic thread onto the bobbin, stretching it slightly. Set the stitch length to 3 mm (about ⅛ in) and test on a piece of scrap fabric. Sometimes the elastic needs to be pulled up after stitching.

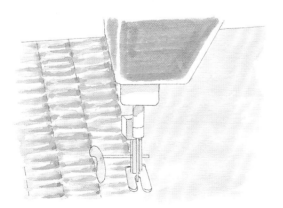

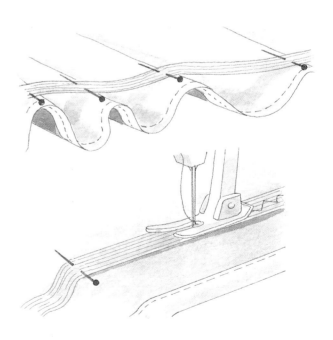

Frills

Hem the frill before attaching it to the seam. Continue as instructed for gathers. Seams may either be overlocked, zigzagged or bound with bias binding.

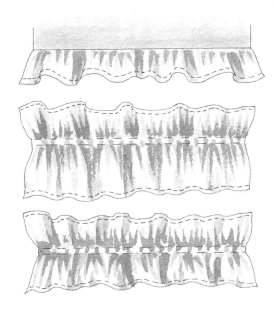

When attaching a frill to a collar, place the frill and the upper collar with right sides facing, and then stitch. Place the under collar on top of the frill, sandwiching the frill in between. The final stitching should be just outside any other stitching so that no previous thread lines show on the completed collar.

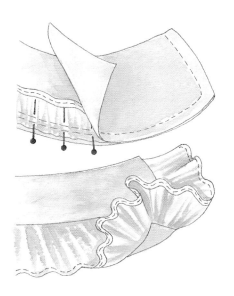

When attaching a double frill, i.e. a frill with a heading, place the wrong side of the frill against the wrong side of the edge, and stitch, frill side up, along the seam line. Trim the seam allowance of the garment to 3 mm (about ⅛ in), turn the frill to the outside of the garment and then topstitch in place along the top row of gathering stitches. The second line of stitching completely encloses the seam allowance. When the frill is not along the edge, gather up the frill, pin in the desired position and topstitch accordingly.

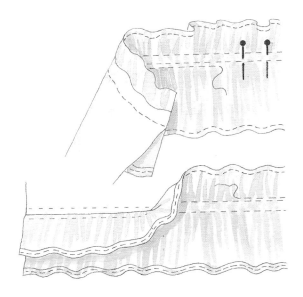

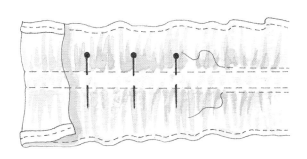

SLITS AND VENTS

Depending on the styling, slits are found in the back or side seams of skirts, tops and jackets. They may be functional, adding extra ease for movement, or they may simply be a design detail. A slit at the centre back of a skirt will expose the leg, but a centre back vent will offer the same ease without exposing the leg. A vent is basically a kick pleat with a slit on the inside. It is used mainly in tailored jackets and coats, two-piece sleeves which are buttoned down at that point, and tailored skirts. For a more professional and expensive look, convert a simple slit into a vent by adding a little extra fabric to the left back seam, as illustrated.

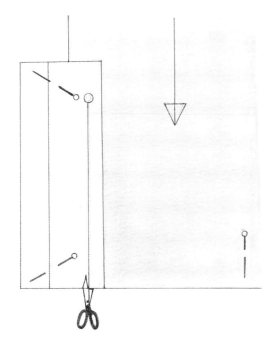

For a crisp, appealing finish, reinforce the crease of the slit or vent with interfacing or strips of double-sided adhesive fusible tape. To prevent a strike through, insert strips of paper between the seam allowance and the garment prior to pressing. Mitring the corners will also contribute to a professional finish.
(Refer to page 40 for mitring.)

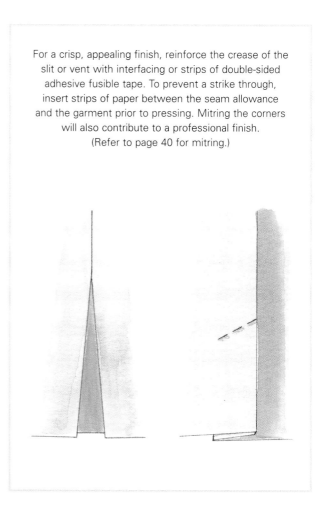

LEFT: Centre front slit

HEMS

Hems should be invisible, unless decorative stitching is required. They should also be smooth, flat and uniform in depth. Use the same shade of thread as the fabric, or slightly darker rather than lighter. There are four basic forms of hems: turned-up, faced, bound and rolled. The depth of the hem will be determined mainly by the design and the fabric used. Except for pleated styles, the marking of the hem is done after the garment has been completed.

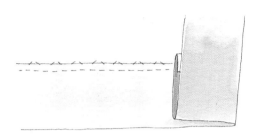

Turned-up Hem

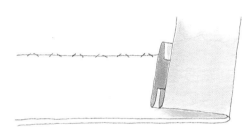

Faced Hem

Bound Hem

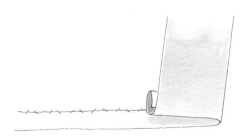

Rolled Hem

Handy hem tips

- Trim the seam allowances of the hem to half the original width.
- Keep shaped and sheer hems narrow. The more they curve, the narrower they should be.
- Straight hems may be deeper, about 3 cm (1¼ in) to 5 cm (2 in), but no more. Very deep hems look unprofessional and decidedly home-made.
- Interface the hems for more weight.
- Narrow hems on soft knits will prevent the garment from sagging.
- Topstitched hems are quick to sew, permanent and add a sporty look.
- When handstitching, use a smaller needle. This way, you are inclined to pick up less fabric with each stitch.
- Be sure to keep your handstitches rather loose to avoid puckering.
- If you want to avoid any stitches showing on the garment, sew the hem to the lining.
- To eliminate the need to colour match the thread to the fabric, use invisible thread.
- Bias-cut and circular skirts need to hang for 24 hours before marking the hem.

Marking the hem

Although the garment's length is mainly determined by the style and current fashion, it should still be flattering to the wearer. Hems can be marked either on a flat surface or on the wearer. Be sure to wear the appropriate undergarments and shoes when marking the hemline of a skirt or dress. Use a hemline marker if there is no one to help you.

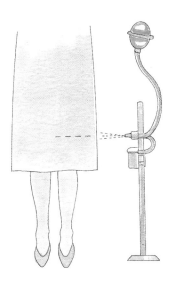

The turned-up hem

This is the most popular type of hem. On a straight edge, this hem presents no problems, but if curved, the fullness needs to be adjusted by easing the edge accordingly. Pull up the ease thread every so often and shrink out the fullness with a steam iron. Before stitching, finish the raw edges of the hem to prevent the fabric from fraying. There are various hem finishes to choose from: pinked, overlocked, turned and stitched, zigzagged and bound edges.

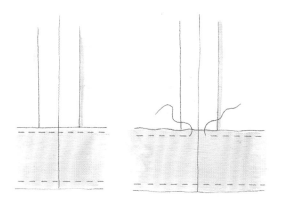

Hem Finishes

PINKED

This edge is suitable for most fabrics which can then be topstiched or fused with double sided tape.

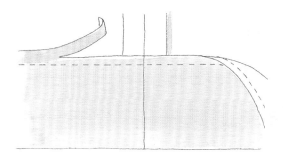

OVERLOCKED

This edge is suitable for all fabrics and is the quickest and tidiest method to use. Any stitching can then be applied.

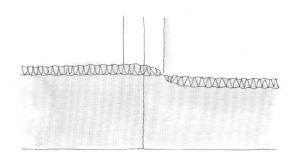

The bound hem, as explained on page 61, is generally favoured by the couturiers.

Turned and stitched

For those who do not own an overlocker, this finish is the neatest to apply to lightweight fabric.

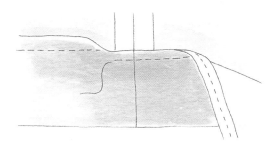

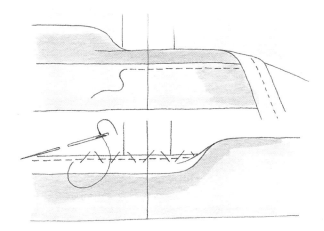

Zigzagged

This finish is appropriate for knits and any fabrics that fray easily, because the stitch gives with the fabric. Trim the edge close to the stitching and hem with a blindstitch.

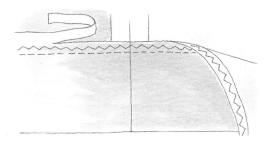

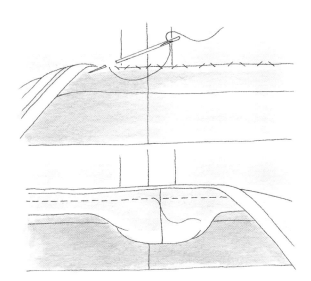

Bound (Hong Kong finish)

This edge is appropriate for heavy woollens and fabrics that fray easily. Finish the raw edge with flat tape or bias binding, woven seam tape for straight hems or stretch lace for curved hems and knits. Hem with a catchstitch or blindstitch in accordance with the weight of the fabric used.

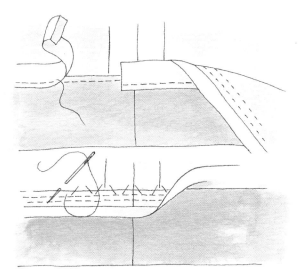

The faced hem

Unusual hem shapes, such as most curved wrap skirts, require a shaped facing. Its use is limited to a hem with minimal flare. Widely flared skirts can, however, be faced with bias binding, if necessary. A bias hem facing may also be used when there is not enough hem allowance to turn up, or if the fabric is exceptionally bulky.

1 If there are no patterns, cut the facings approximately 6 cm (2⅜ in) wide to fit along the hemline. Join the pieces, press the seams open and then trim the seam allowance by half. Finish the inner edge selecting one of the finishes discussed on pages 60–61.

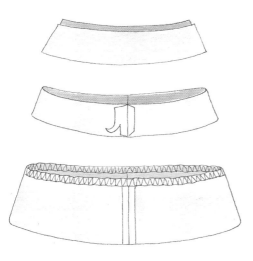

2 Attach the facing, trim the seam and notch the seam allowance, if necessary.

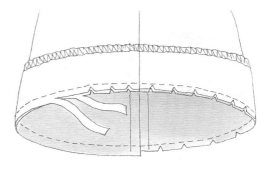

3 Press the seams open, and then towards the facing. Understitch close to the seam edge through all the seams.

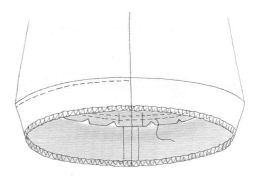

4 Turn the facing inside the garment and press the hemline. It should be 3 mm (⅛ in) from the fold. Stitch the hem down using the appropriate stitch.

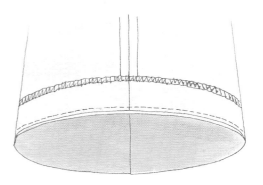

5 For bias facings, follow the same method but join the strips on the bias.

A bias strip can be stretched or shrunk into shape using a steam iron. This should be done before attaching the facing to the garment.

The bound hem

A strip of binding is used to encase the hem edge. This neat and practical finish is ideal for reversible garments. The binding may be of woven fabric (cut on the bias) or knit (cut on the cross grain). Folded braid, bias binding or petersham ribbon can also be used and are most attractive, especially in contrasting colours and textures.

SINGLE BINDING

1 Cut bias strips four times the finished width of the binding and the length of the edge plus 5 cm (2 in) for ease and joining.

2 With the wrong sides facing, fold the bias strip in half lengthwise and press lightly, taking care not to stretch the fabric.

3 Open out the binding and fold the edges to meet at the centre crease. Press, shaping the binding if necessary.

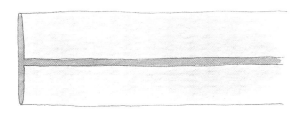

4 Open out one fold and pin the binding to the hem edge with right sides facing and raw edges together. Turn back the starting end by 1 cm (⅜ in), aligning it with the garment seam. Stitch to within about 8 cm (3⅛ in) of the starting point.

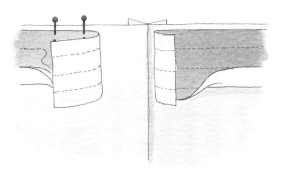

5 Trim the excess binding allowing 1 cm (⅜ in) to overlap the starting end. Continue stitching the rest of the way across through all the thicknesses.

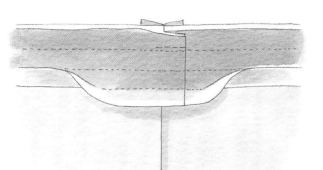

6 Press the seam allowances towards the binding and fold the binding in half on the pressed line.

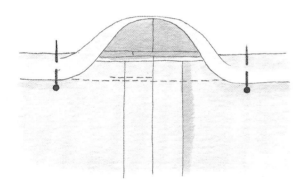

7 For a woven binding, line up the turned-under edge with the seam line, pin in place and slip-stitch the hem as well as the binding ends by hand.

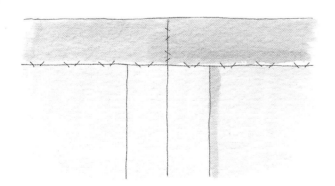

8 For a knitted binding, machine stitch on the right side in the groove of the seam. Trim the excess binding and slipstitch the binding ends.

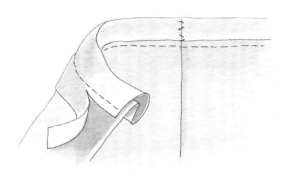

Topstitched single binding

1 Fold the strip lengthwise a little off centre so that the one side is about 3 mm (⅛ in) wider than the other side and press lightly.

2 Open out the binding and then fold the edges to meet at the crease. Press, shaping the binding if necessary.

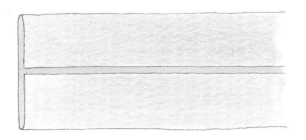

3 With the right side up, wrap the binding over the hem edge, with the wider side on the inside of the garment. Position the starting end 1 cm (⅜ in) beyond the garment seam and then pin the binding. Stitch on the right side to within about 8 cm (3⅛ in) of the starting point.

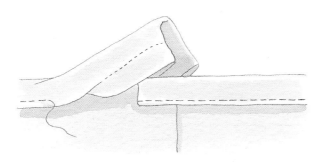

4 Trim the excess binding, allowing about 2 cm (¾ in) to overlap the starting end. Fold the second end under for 1 cm (⅜ in) and lap it over the first one, aligning the second fold with the garment seam, as illustrated.

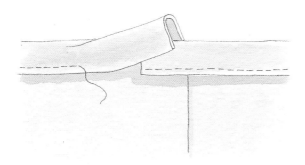

5 Tuck in the edges neatly and continue stitching the rest of the way across. Finally, slipstitch the ends of the binding.

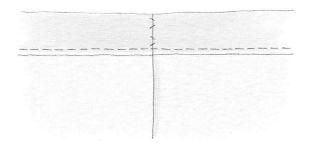

Save time by using a binding attachment on your sewing machine. Simply cut the binding and feed it through the binder as you attach it to your hem. Trim, tuck the end back and slipstitch.

The rolled hem

This fine hem is suitable for sheer, delicate fabrics. There are two handstitched methods favoured by the couturiers. Both are time-consuming but well worth the effort. However, the machine method is faster and only requires the knack of holding and feeding the fabric into the rolled hem foot.

Double-turn the hem and sew a few stitches to hold the fold. With the needle down, insert the folded fabric into the spiral of the foot. Lower the foot and start stitching, holding the fabric at an angle to the left and slightly taut.

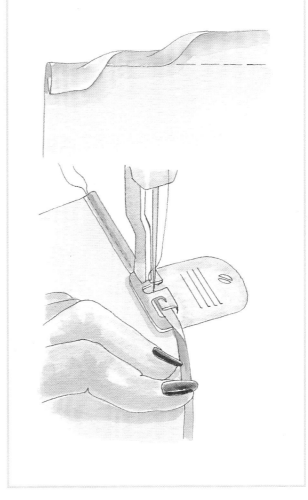

HAND-ROLLED METHOD 1

Machine stitch 6 mm (¼ in) from the raw edge and trim close to the stitching. Roll about 3 mm (⅛ in) of the edge between the thumb and forefinger, concealing the stitching. Stabilize the roll with the third and fourth finger and slipstitch, taking a single thread in each stitch.

HAND-ROLLED METHOD 2

Stitch and trim as above. Turn in the edge about 3 mm (⅛ in) and crease sharply. Pick up a thread along the crease, then carry the thread over to the raw edge diagonally and pick up a thread alongside the raw edge. Work in a zigzag pattern, making the stitches 6 mm (¼ in) apart. Repeat the process for about 2.5 cm (1 in), then pull the thread to tighten the stitches, thereby creating the roll.

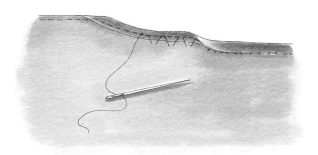

Hemming a lining

Linings can be hemmed in two ways: they can be sewn to the garment with a fold provided for easy movement, or they can be hemmed separately and secured to the garment with French tacks. The sewn-in linings are suitable for jacket and waistcoat hems as well as for sleeves. The loose linings are appropriate for skirts, dresses and coats. Prior to hemming the lining, the garment hem should be finished and the lining sewn in place except for the last 15 cm (6 in). Smooth down the lining and pin to the garment all round at the 15 cm (6 in) mark.

ATTACHED LINING

1 Trim the lining to 1.5 cm (⅝ in) below the finished garment edge. If the hem needs easing, easestitch 1 cm (⅜ in) from that edge.

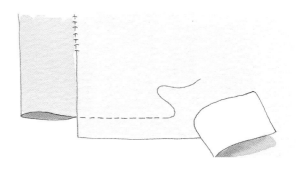

2 Turn back the lining about 2.5 cm (1 in) so that the fold is 1 cm (⅜ in) from the garment edge. Pin the lining to the garment, placing the pins 1 cm (⅜ in) above and parallel to the fold.

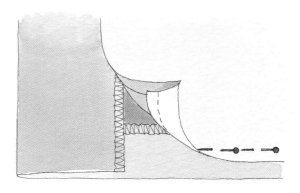

RIGHT: The hems of this double-layered chiffon dress have been rolled and zigzagged by machine to create a 'lettuce edge'.

3 Fold the lining back along the pinned line and slipstitch it to the garment hem, catching the underlayer of the lining only.

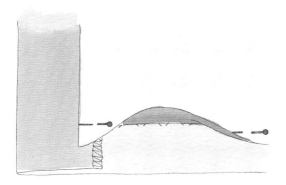

4 Remove pins and press lining fold lightly. Slipstitch the remaining lining edges to the facing.

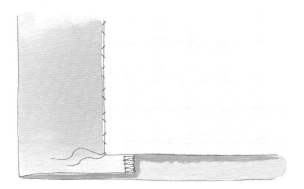

LOOSE LINING

1 Trim the lining so that the amount left is equal to the lining hem allowance minus 2.5 cm (1 in). That is, for a 5 cm (2 in) hem, the lining would be trimmed to 2.5 cm (1 in) below the garment.

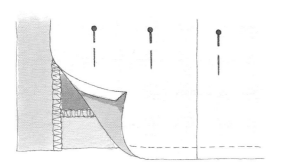

2 Turn back the lining so that the fold is 2.5 cm (1 in) from the garment hem. Pin the lining close to the fold, ensuring that the hem allowance is an even width.

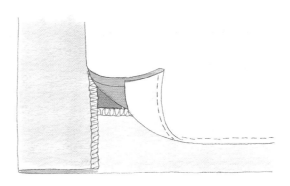

3 Ease the edge if necessary and hem, using the appropriate stitch. A machine stitch will suffice.

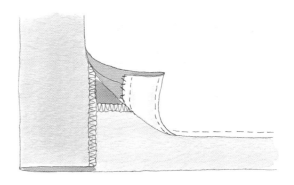

4 Attach the lining to the garment with 2 cm (⅞ in) French tacks, placing one at each seam. Slipstitch the remaining lining edges to the facing.

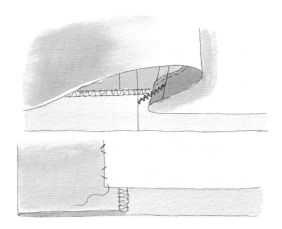

PLACKETS

A placket is a lightweight finish which provides a secure closing. This finish is applied to a sleeve at the cuff opening and to a partial opening at the neck where it is usually buttoned closed. The three most popular finishes are the faced placket, the continuous-bound placket and the shirt placket. All three are applicable to the sleeve and the neck. A separate buttonstand on a blouse or shirt is also referred to as a placket. A buttonstand may have a facing which is folded back, but this can be altered slightly to simulate a separate or even a concealed buttonstand.

Faced placket

1 Cut a rectangular facing 6.5 cm (2½ in) wide and 2.5 cm (1 in) longer than the required slit. Overlock or double-turn three of the edges, leaving the bottom one raw. With right sides facing, centre the facing over the marked opening and pin in position. Stitch from the edge to the point, pivot and stitch back to the edge. Press flat.

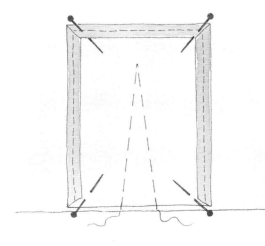

2 Slash to the point, being sure not to cut the thread, turn the facing to the wrong side of the sleeve. Press flat and slipstitch the facing down.

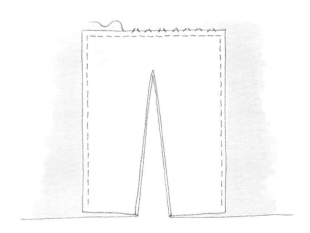

Continuous-bound placket

1 Cut self bias binding 3 cm (1¼ in) wide and twice the length of the marked slit. Press one side 6 mm (¼ in) under to the wrong side and mark a 6 mm (¼ in) seam along the other side.

2 Reinforce the placket opening by staystitching from the edge to the point, pivoting and stitching back to the edge. Slash to the point.

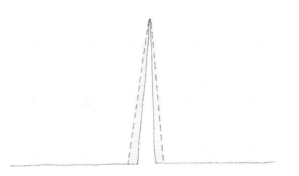

3 With right sides facing, pin the unfolded edge of the binding to the sleeve, aligning the reinforced stitching with the marked seam line. Stitch, with the sleeve side up, and press the seam flat.

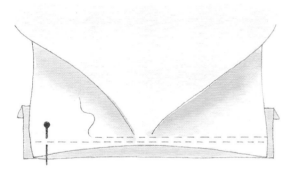

4 Fold the binding over to the wrong side, encasing the raw edges. Line up the folded edge with the stitching line, pin in place and slipstitch. Turn the front edge of the binding to the wrong side of the sleeve and press.

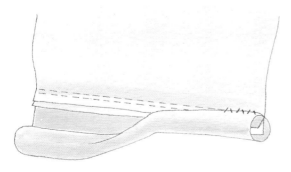

This method can be simplified by feeding the bias strip through a binder and attaching it to the sleeve at the same time, as explained on page 65.

Shirt placket

1 Fold the overlap in half with right sides facing, pin and stitch around the top edge to the matching point at the side. Press seam flat, trim the seam allowance and clip at the matching point. Turn to the right side, pull out the corners and press flat. Press under the seam allowance along the top edge.

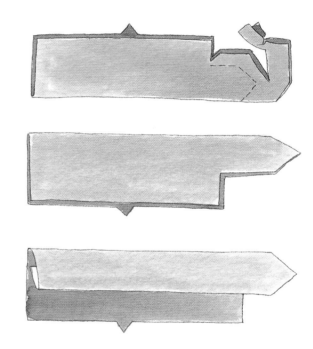

2 Press the seam allowance on the one side of the underlap to the wrong side and trim this seam to about half its width.

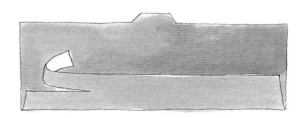

3 Reinforce the placket opening by staystitching 1 cm (⅜ in) away from the marked slit all round, as illustrated. Slash to within 1 cm (⅜ in) of the placket top and then to the corners. Determine the front and back edges of the opening.

5 Press the seam allowance towards the underlap, fold the underlap towards the right side and pin the folded edge over the stitching line. Edgestitch through all the layers, stop at the corner and secure the stitches.

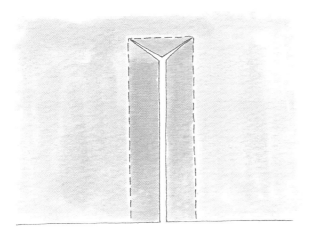

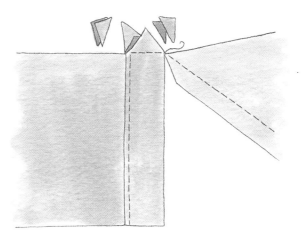

4 Pin and stitch the right side of the unfolded underlap edge to the wrong side of the back placket edge, aligning the seam lines. Secure the stitches at the top corner of the placket, then press flat and trim.

6 Flip up the triangular piece at the top of the placket and pin it to the underlap. Stitch across the base of the triangle, securing the stitches at the beginning and at the end. Trim the square corners of the underlap.

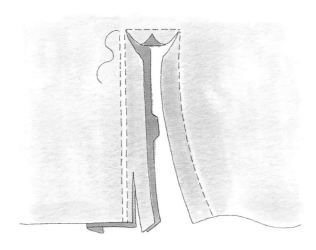

7 Pin and stitch the right side of the unfolded overlap edge to the wrong side of the front placket edge, aligning the seam lines. Secure the stitches at the top.

9 Pin the top portion of the overlap to the sleeve, covering the top portion of the underlap and tack down, if necessary.

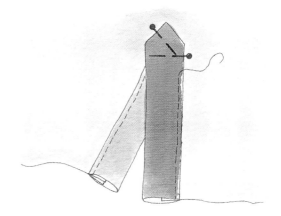

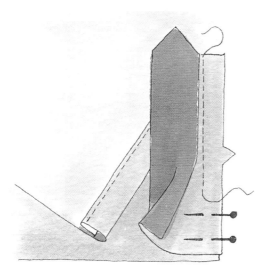

10 Topstitch along the folded edge of the over-lap, but be sure not to catch the underlap in the stitching. Stop stitching at the end of the placket opening, then pull the threads through to the wrong side and knot.

8 Press the seam flat, trim the seam allowance to half its width and press again towards the overlap. Bring the folded edge of the overlap to the stitching line and pin in place.

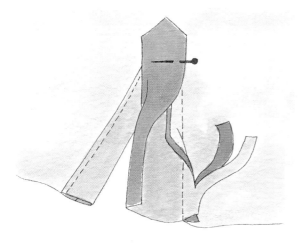

11 Topstitch through all the layers across the overlap, around the pointed end and down to the sleeve edge. Remove any tacking and press.

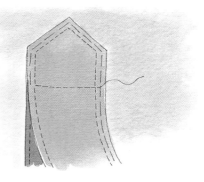

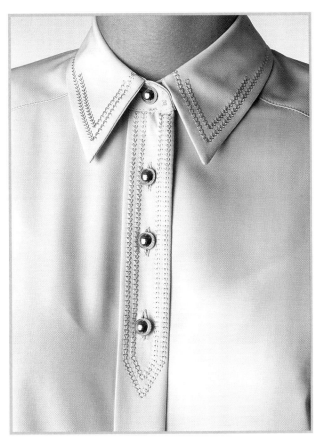
Partly concealed placket

Half placket on a knitted T-shirt

Shirt sleeve placket

Basic shirt placket

Straight placket band

1 Reinforce the placket opening by staystitching 1 cm (⅜ in) away from the slit all round, as illustrated. Slash to within 1 cm (⅜ in) of the placket bottom and then to the corners.

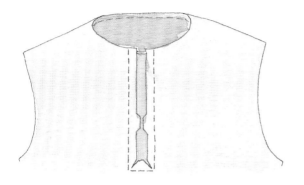

2 Fuse the placket bands as required and, with wrong sides facing, fold the band in half lengthwise and press flat.

3 With right sides together, pin each placket to the opening, aligning the edges, and tack if necessary. Stitch through all the layers, stopping 1 cm (⅜ in) from the bottom edge.

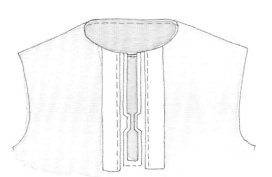

For a collarless garment, stitch the top ends of both plackets, trim, turn to the right side and then press.

4 Flip up the triangular piece at the bottom of the opening and pin to both the placket ends, taking care to keep the right placket over the left one. Stitch across to secure the plackets.

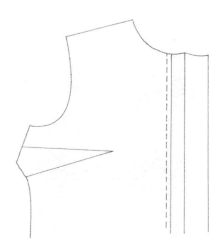

5 Overlock the necessary edges, then turn to the right side and press.

False placket

This example has a 3 cm (1¼ in) wide placket.

1 Shift the centre front over by 3 mm (⅛ in) to allow for the tuck. Mark the fold line parallel to the new centre front and 1.5 cm (⅝ in) away. Mark the edge of the facing 3 cm (1¼ in) away.

2 Fuse the facing with a suitable interfacing and press back along the fold line. Fold the front back again by the same amount so that the raw edge is encased, just touching the inside of the second fold.

Concealed placket

This example also has a 3 cm (1¼ in) wide placket.

1 Mark the first fold line 1.5 cm (⅝ in) from the centre front; mark the next fold line 3 cm (1¼ in) from the first; mark the third fold line 2.7 cm (1⅛ in) from the second; and mark the fourth fold line 2.7 cm (1⅛ in) from the third. Add 6 mm (¼ in) for the seam allowance. Fuse a strip of interfacing between the third and fourth folds.

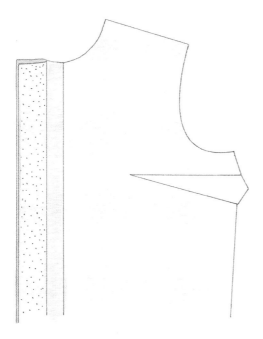

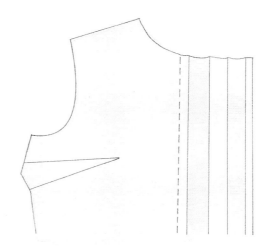

3 With the wrong side of the blouse facing up, stitch a 3 mm (⅛ in) tuck along this fold line. This topstitching will ultimately be on the upper side of the placket. Flip the folded edge back and press the edge towards the side seam. Topstitch the outer edge 3 mm (⅛ in) away from the fold.

2 Fold the third line over towards the wrong side and press. Then fold the first line over towards the wrong side and press. With right side up, stitch 3 cm (1¼ in) from the first fold line, through all the layers and encasing the raw edge, i.e. along the second fold line. Fold the under placket out towards the garment edge. The buttons and buttonholes will be on this under placket. In this way, the buttonstand is concealed by the top placket.

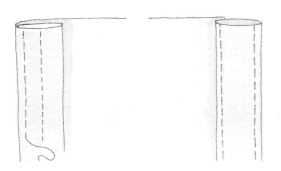

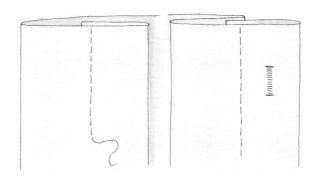

BUTTONHOLES

Buttons are an important finishing touch and need to be chosen with care. They should relate to the fabric and design of the garment. Spacing and proportion are important, as is ensuring that buttons are placed at all the strategic points of stress.

The choice of buttonhole is also significant. There are two basic types of buttonholes: worked, which can be done either by machine or by hand, and bound, which are time-consuming but add a tailored and professional look to all garments. The latter is preferred by the couturiers.

In-seam buttonhole

Bound buttonhole

Positioning buttonholes

Before positioning the buttonholes, you need to determine their length. This must be done accurately to allow the button to pass through easily, yet hold the garment securely closed. The length of the buttonhole equals the diameter of the button plus its height. This applies to a bound buttonhole, but

3 mm (⅛ in) must be added to a worked buttonhole because of the finishing at each end.

Test the buttonhole length by first slashing a piece of scrap fabric from the actual garment to the required length and then by constructing a sample buttonhole on this scrap . The overlap (the distance from button position to fold) is usually 1.5 cm (⅝ in) on a regular pattern. If the diameter of the button measures more than that, the overlap will need to be extended accordingly, as illustrated.

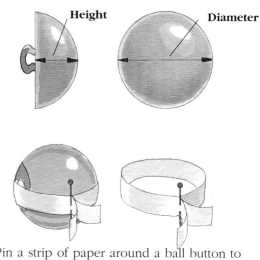

Pin a strip of paper around a ball button to determine the buttonhole length

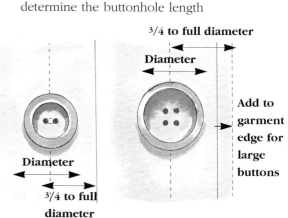

Horizontal buttonholes

Horizontal buttonholes are the most secure kind, as the pull of the closure is absorbed by the end of the buttonhole. They are, therefore, used on most types of garments. The buttons are placed on the placement line (which is usually the centre front), but the buttonholes must extend 3 mm (⅛ in) beyond this line, as illustrated.

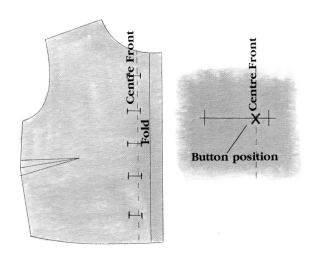

Vertical buttonholes

Vertical buttonholes are only used on separate or stitched-down buttonstands, such as those on shirts, or where many small buttons are involved. The buttons are placed on the placement line and the buttonholes are marked directly on this line, with the top of the buttonhole 3 mm (⅛ in) above the centre of the button, as illustrated.

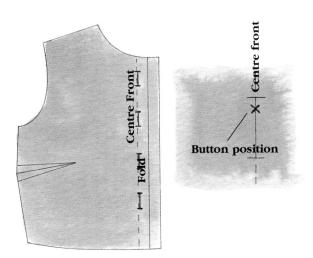

Buttonhole positioning

In women's garments, buttonholes are placed on the right-hand side of the garment on the front and on the left-hand side at the back. On mens' shirts and jackets, however, the buttonholes are placed on the left-hand side. The first buttonhole below the collar should be placed as close to the top as possible, about 2.5 cm (1 in) down. The next buttonhole to mark should be the one in line with the bust point for ladies or the underarm for men. The rest can then be spaced evenly between these two. A button needs to be placed at the waistline of a dress to prevent gaping. The spacing between each buttonhole should be about 8 cm (3⅛ in), and the last one should be about 10 cm (4 in) to 12 cm (5 in) from the bottom of the garment. Only cardigans have buttons right at the bottom. On double-breasted garments, the two rows of buttons must be equidistant from the centre front line. Mark the buttonholes to correspond with each row of buttons.

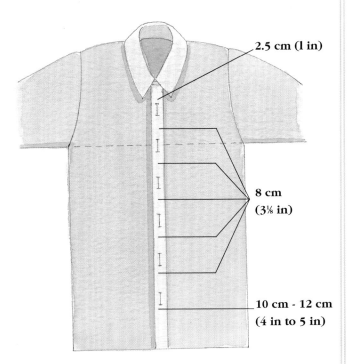

Machine-worked buttonholes

These buttonholes consist of two parallel rows of zigzag stitches, with both ends bartacked to prevent the hole from tearing. Most sewing machines have a special buttonhole attachment or built-in capabilities which can be set to the desired size. The buttonhole is slashed open after the stitching is completed. These buttonholes are used in most garments, as this is by far the quickest method.

Hand-worked buttonholes

These buttonholes are used mainly on tailored garments and on fabrics too sheer for bound buttonholes. A cut is edged with hand buttonhole stitches and the ends finished off with bartacks or a fan-shaped arrangement of stitches.

Bound buttonholes

Bound buttonholes must be made before attaching the facing. They are made from strips of fabric, cut either on the straight or on the bias, which are folded into two narrow welts, measuring 3 mm (⅛ in) in width, and are then set into a rectangular opening. Cut one continuous strip of fabric for all the buttonholes, allowing an extra 2.5 cm (1 in) per buttonhole.

> Complete the same step on all the buttonholes before proceeding to the next step. Machine tack all markings using polyester thread; be sure to loosen the tension slightly. For permanent stitching, use a fine stitch (about 15 to 20 stitches per 2.5 cm [1 in]).

ONE-PIECE FOLDED METHOD

This simple method is easy to follow and only requires one fabric strip per buttonhole. Accuracy and uniformity will result in a professional finish. Should the buttonhole seem limp and somewhat thin, draw wool or soft cord into the welts before the triangular ends of the buttonhole are stitched together, as illustrated.

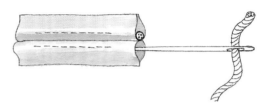

1 Before constructing the buttonholes, mark both ends and the centre of each one very accurately by machine tacking.

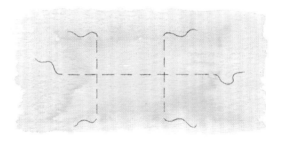

2 Cut a strip 2.5 cm (1 in) wide and as long as required, remembering to add an extra 2.5 cm (1 in) per buttonhole. Fuse only if fabric frays. Cut the strip into the required lengths per buttonhole.

3 With wrong sides together, fold and press the patch in half lengthwise, marking the centre with a crease. With right sides together, centre the crease of the patch directly over the buttonhole markings and machine tack.

4 Fold and press the long raw edges of the patch so that they meet at the centre tacking line. Using a fine stitch length, stitch through the exact centre of each half of the patch, starting and stopping exactly on the markings for the ends of the buttonholes.

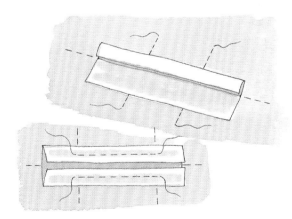

5 Pull the threads to the wrong side and tie. (Do not backstitch as this may inadvertently go off the stitching line.) Remove the tacking threads and press. Cut through the centre of the patch to form two welts, taking care not to cut through the garment fabric underneath the patch. Turn to the wrong side, cut along the centre line and then into each corner, just short of the stitching, as illustrated.

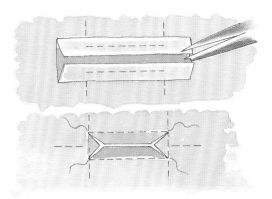

6 Carefully push the welts through the opening to the wrong side and adjust them to square off the corners. Tack the welts together diagonally by hand and press.

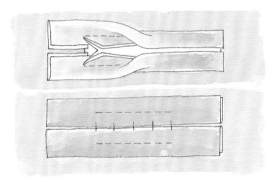

7 Place the garment on the machine, with right side up, and fold back the fabric just enough to expose one of the triangular buttonhole ends. Stitch back and forth along this line to secure it to the welts. Repeat at the other end.

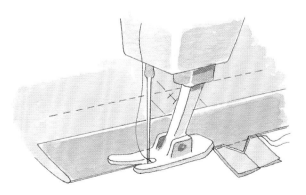

8 Remove any remaining tacking threads, trim the welt ends to 6 mm (¼ in) and press them with the tip of the iron.

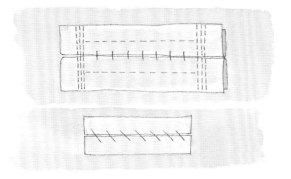

OVAL FACING FINISH

1 Once the buttonholes have been made, attach the facings. Open and finish off the area behind the buttonhole. Press the facing flat and pin around each buttonhole to prevent the layers from slipping. Mark the buttonhole opening by inserting a pin at each end of the buttonhole.

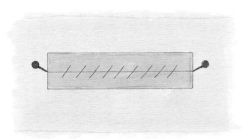

2 Turn to the facing side and slash between the pins. Ensure that the slash is not longer than the buttonhole and that it falls, preferably, on the straight grain. Remove the pins.

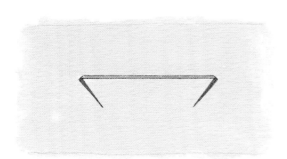

3 Carefully turn the edges of the slash under, enough to clear the opening of the buttonhole. Slip-hem the facing in place around the buttonhole, being very careful not to allow any stitches to show on the right side.

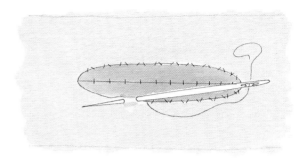

RECTANGULAR FACING FINISH

1 Press the facing flat and then secure it in position by pinning around each buttonhole. Insert a pin at each corner of the buttonhole through to the facing side.

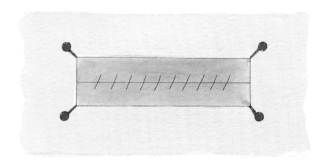

2 Turn to the facing side and cut along the centre of this pinned area and then into each corner, just short of the pins. Remove the pins.

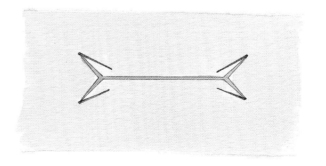

3 Carefully turn back the edges on all four sides and align with the buttonhole. Slip-hem the facing to the back of the buttonhole.

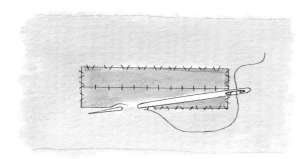

Button loops

Button loops can be substituted for buttonholes, provided they are suitable to the style of the garment. They work particularly well on lace where minimal handling should be used. Ball buttons and buttons with shanks fit best and are preferable to use. Patterns might need adjusting as these loops are attached at the edge of the garment and therefore do not need the overlap on the upper side. Attach a loop and button to a piece of scrap to test for size and security and also to check whether the diameter of the loop is suitable for the button size. Cord is also available and is quick and easy to attach.

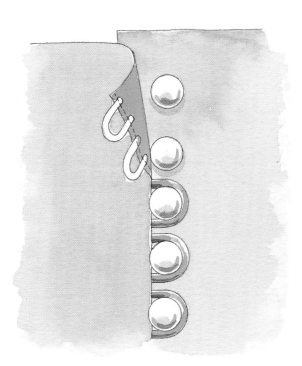

SPAGHETTI (ROULEAU) TUBING

1 Cut bias strips 2.7 cm (1⅛ in) wide. Fold in half lengthwise with right sides together and stitch 6 mm (¼ in) from the fold. For a narrower spaghetti, stitch 3 mm (⅛ in) from the fold and trim off excess so that a 3 mm (⅛ in) to 5 mm (³⁄₁₆ in) seam remains.

2 Thread a bodkin or large needle with a heavy duty thread and fasten the thread at one end of the tubing. Insert the needle, eye first, into the tubing. Pull the needle through the tube with one hand and manipulate the fabric with moistened fingers of the other hand to turn the tube into itself. Work the needle all the way through until the entire tube is turned to the right side.

Button loops substituted for buttonholes.

CORDED SPAGHETTI (ROULEAU) TUBING

1 Cut bias strips equal to the diameter of the cord used plus 2.5 cm (1 in) and cut the cord twice as long as the bias.

2 Fold the bias strips around one half of the length of the cord, with right sides together. Using a zip foot, first stitch across the end of the bias at the centre of the cord, and then stitch down the length of the bias, close to the cord, stretching the bias slightly.

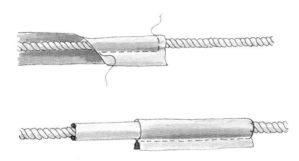

3 Trim the seam allowances and then turn the bias tube to the right side by drawing the enclosed cord out of the tube. The free end will automatically go into the tube. Finally trim the excess cord and the stitched end.

For bulky fabrics it is necessary to extend a shank or attach a sew-through button forming a shank. Lay a matchstick or toothpick across the button and sew the button down, then remove the stick and wind the thread firmly around the stitches to make the shank.

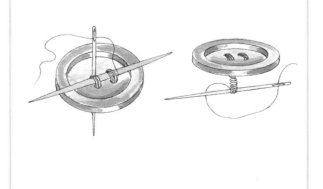

Buttons

As previously discussed, buttons for horizontal buttonholes are placed 3 mm (⅛ in) away from the end of the buttonhole closest to the edge of the garment. Buttons for vertical buttonholes are placed 3 mm (⅛ in) down from the top of a buttonhole. Having made the buttonholes, mark the button position accordingly.

There are two types of buttons: shank, with a little loop or 'neck', and regular sew-through buttons. Shanks are mainly used on jackets and coats and where heavier fabric is required. Sew-through buttons are popular in most areas.

Buttons have been used to create a military effect.

Buttons are usually attached by hand, though some sewing machines do have this facility. At points of strain, a reinforcing button can be stitched behind the button on the inside of the garment to prevent the button from tearing through the fabric.

Snap fastener

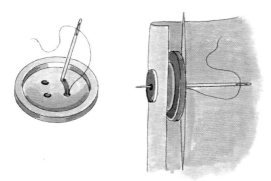

Commercial fasteners

Hooks and eyes, as well as snap fasteners, are usually attached by hand and used where buttons would be unsuitable. These are both available on continuous tape. Hook and loop tape, such as Velcro, is a good alternative.

Snap fastener tape requires a double seam allowance for the underlap. Hook and loop tape (Velcro) also calls for a lapped application. Hook and eye tape, however, requires a centred application. With tape fasteners closed, position tape at the garment opening and pin in position on both sides of tape. In this way, the fasteners will be correctly aligned. Unfasten and stitch around all the edges, ensuring that the needle does not hit any metal parts.

Snap fastener tape is suitable for infants' clothes; hook and eye tape is used where greater strain is exerted on the garment, such as with bustiers and corsetry; and Velcro is becoming more popular and is widely used on clothing, footwear and luggage. It is both strong and easy to handle.

Snap fastener tape

Hook and loop tape (Velcro)

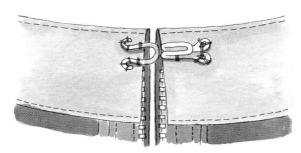

Hook and eye

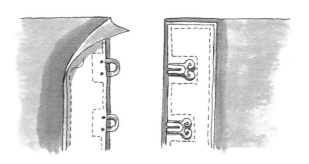

Hook and eye tape

ZIPS

Whitcomb L. Judson of Chicago was the first person to hit upon the idea of the zip-fastener in 1891. Hooks and eyes were mounted on a pair of small chains with a sliding clasp which automatically fastened them. But the final triumph came in 1923, when the BF Goodrich Company used a similar gadget on their rubber galoshes. The company president called for a name containing the word 'zip'.

Since then, zips have become lighter, less obvious and more supple, and are used to close an amazing variety of fashion features. Zips are available in numerous colours, lengths and weights, and have either metal or plastic teeth. The zip tapes are woven from nylon, polyester, cotton or cotton blend. They may be closed or open-ended and they come with a variety of sliders.

Exposed zips on fronts, pockets and cuffs can add an interesting detail to a simple garment.

Zips can be shortened by whipstitching at the required length and then trimming off the excess. Seam allowances can be increased to facilitate the insertion of a zip by adding a piece of tape to the seam. Trim cross-seams to reduce bulk. There are various applications, the most popular being centred, lapped and fly-front.

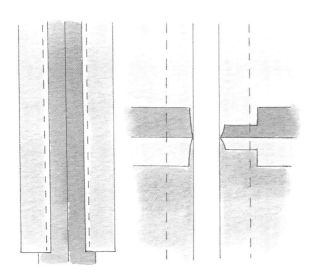

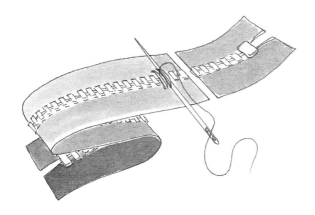

Increased seam allowance

Trim cross-seams to reduce bulk

Centred zip

This application is used at the centre front and back of a garment and at the edges of sleeves. Tacking the seam closed prior to attaching the zip is optional, although not infallible. Aligning the folded edge of the opening with the teeth will, however, ensure that the teeth are not exposed.

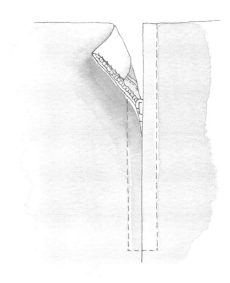

1 Stitch the seam, leaving the opening for the zip. Fold the seam allowances under and press.

2 Place the zip face down and position it about 6 mm (¼ in) to 1 cm (⅜ in) below the seam line at the top. Ensure that the bottom stopper is just below the opening at the bottom. This will compel you to stitch across the zip above the metal stopper, securing the end and preventing needle breakage. Pin in position.

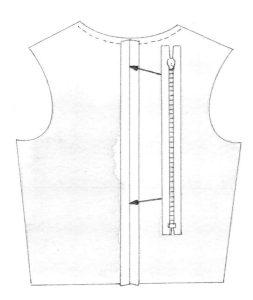

3 With the right side of the garment facing up and the zip closed, stitch across the bottom of the zip and up the one side. Open the zip slightly to stitch past the slider, as explained on page 85 (see box). Move the zip foot to the other side and then stitch across the bottom and up along the other side in the same manner. Ensure that the folded edge covers the teeth at all times. Pull the threads through to the wrong side and secure.

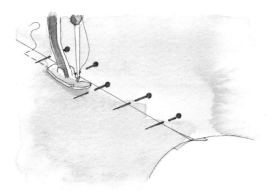

Apply glue stick or basting tape, instead of pins, to hold the zip in position. Use a 2 cm (³/₄ in) transparent tape as a guide for topstitching the zip.

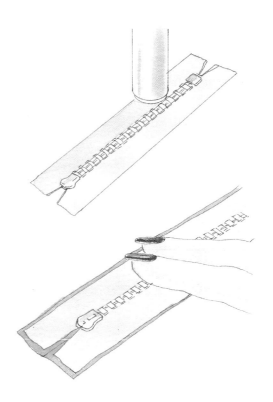

Pins are seldom used in the commercial trade to hold pieces of fabric together. In some cases machine tacking is used, but seamstresses rely mainly on notches in seams and their own experience when constructing a garment.

Lapped zip

A lapped zip is used on skirts, trousers and dresses. This application is especially suited to zips inserted in side seams. It is advisable to position the zip below the seam line at the top and just below the opening at the bottom, as instructed for the centred zip. To simplify the installation of this zip, use a slightly larger seam allowance on the lap or right side and use a guide when topstitching.

2 With the right side of the garment facing up and the zip open, place the zip face down on the garment, with the teeth on the pressed seam line. Pin in position and stitch from the bottom to the top. Close the zip and fold the seam allowance back.

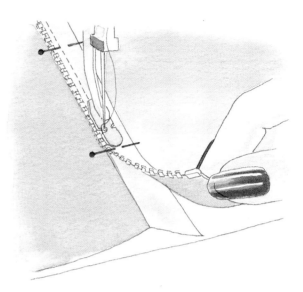

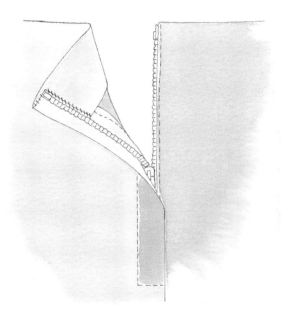

3 Position the pressed seam allowance on the free side of the zip so that the fold overlaps the teeth. Pin or glue in place and stitch across the bottom and up the side, pivoting at the corner and using a guide for the topstitching. Pull the threads through to the wrong side and secure.

1 Stitch the seam, leaving an opening for the zip. Fold the seam allowances under and press.

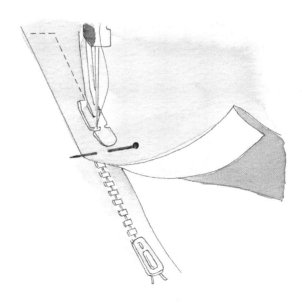

Fly-front

This application is traditionally used on men's trousers but because of its neat closing, it is popular on women's clothing as well, where it laps right over left. In men's garments it laps left over right. Most zip types are suitable; metal zips are, however, preferable in heavy trousers, such as jeans.

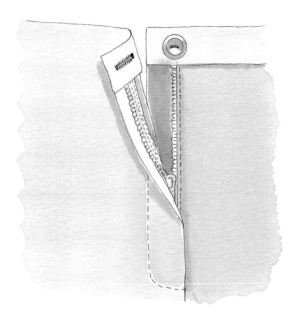

1 With right sides together, stitch the fly facing to the right front. Overlock the edges of this facing and the crotch as well as the left front crotch.

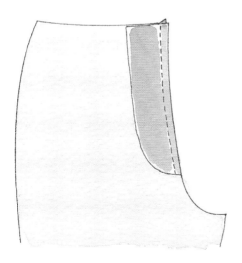

2 Press the seam flat, so that the edges face the garment, and align the zip, facing down, with the seam line. Pin in place and, using the zip foot, stitch from the top downwards, close to the teeth.

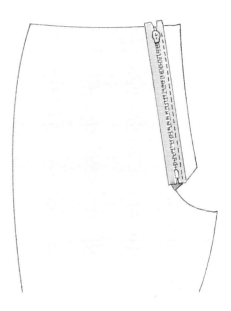

3 Stitch the bottom seam of the placket, then turn to the right side and press. Overlock the vertical edge of the placket.

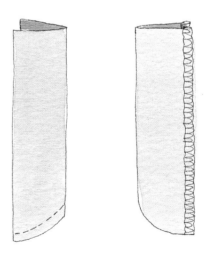

RIGHT: The fly-fronts on girls- and womenswear lap right over left, whereas on boys- and menswear they lap left over right as shown here.

4 First place the placket with the overlocked edge to the right hand side, then position the other side of the zip, facing upwards, on top of the placket. Lastly, position the left front, right side down, on top of the zip. Ensure that all the edges are aligned, pin in place and stitch.

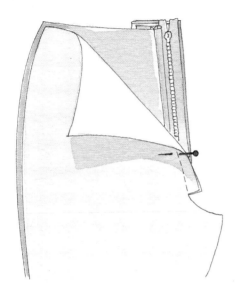

5 Turn over and stitch the crotch from the bottom at the inside leg to just beyond the seam line of the fly and then backstitch.

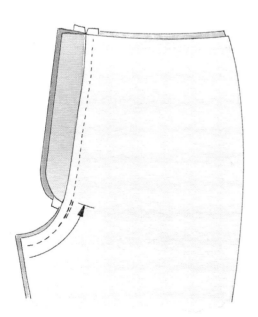

6 Turn the garment to the right side, fold the fly back on the seam line and press. Secure the fly with pins, keeping the placket aside to prevent it being caught in the stitching. Mark the fly with tailor's chalk and topstitch. Reinforce the bottom of the fly, vertically, with a bartack.

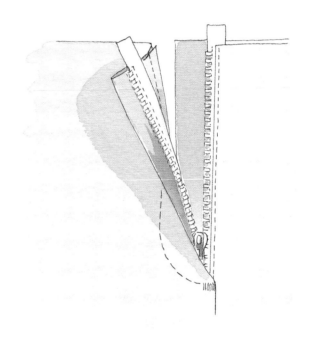

A man's fly-front is constructed using the same method, except that the left and right sides need to be exchanged. The fly facing and placket may require interfacing, depending on the weight of the fabric used.

'Denim is the one thing everyone owns.'

Donna Karan

Invisible zip

This zip is different from the conventional zip and, when closed, it seems to disappear into the seam exposing only the tab. A special zip foot is available for this application, although the regular zip foot will suffice. Press the coils of the zip slightly upwards to facilitate the insertion. An invisible zip must be applied to an open seam and stitched only to the seam allowances.

Exposed zip

This zip is usually applied on sweatshirts and other knitted garments where there is no seam. The opening needs to be reinforced with interfacing. This is then slashed along the centre line to within 1 cm (⅜ in) of the bottom, and cut into the corners. The zip can be inserted on the wrong side, flipping the triangular piece down at the bottom. Having done this, the right side of the garment can now be topstitched, as desired.

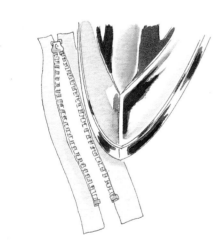

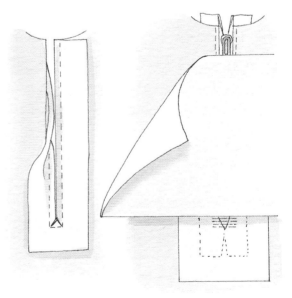

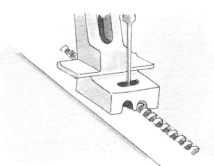

FINISHES

Donna Karan once said: 'How the clothes relate to the body and how they move with the woman is what's important.' A garment should lie smoothly and neatly around the neck and across the shoulders; sleeves should be comfortable and set in correctly; waistbands should be well constructed and fit snugly but not too tightly; and pockets need to be perfectly aligned and stitched with care. Everything you do in sewing counts in the creation of a better-fitting, better-looking, longer-wearing item of clothing. Adhering to these principal factors will always result in the undeniable elegance of a Parisian gown.

NECKLINES

The neckline is a focal point on most garments. It is important to select a finish that flatters the face and highlights your best features, while drawing attention away from the worst. For this reason, maternity garments often have decorative necklines.

Facings must be snipped or notched, especially at the corners, to prevent puckering; collars must be symmetrical, attached impeccably and fit smoothly; in fact, all neckline finishes require trimming and understitching for a successful result.

Facings

A facing is used to finish raw edges. It is attached to the edge, turned to the inside of the garment and should not show on the outside. Most facings require interfacing to define, support and reinforce the shape of the neck.

> In the commercial trade, the facing is attached to the neck, the zip is first attached to the facing, and then attached to the garment opening. In this way, all handwork is eliminated.

Single neck facing

1 Fuse the interfacing to the wrong side of the facing, if required. Join the shoulder seams and then press open.

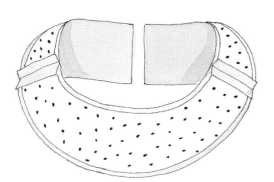

2 Overlock, pink or turn-and-stitch the raw edges of the facing. With right sides together, pin the facing to the garment, matching any notches and seam lines. If the zip has already been inserted, open the zip and wrap the ends around each side of the zip to the inside.

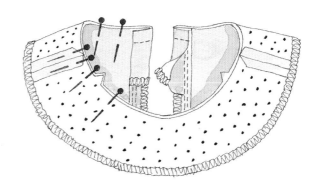

> Stitch in the seam line, often referred to as 'stitch in the ditch', to minimise time-consuming hand tacking.

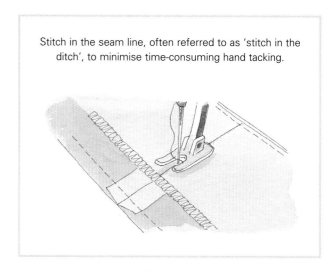

3 Stitch together. Trim and grade the seam allowances, keeping the garment seam allowances the widest. Trim the centre back corners diagonally as well as the cross-seam allowances at the shoulders. Clip the curved seam allowances. For square necklines, be sure to reinforce the corners before clipping into them.

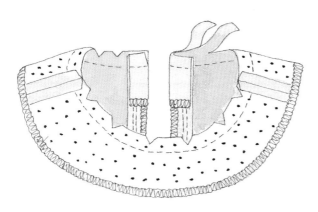

4 With the wrong side up, press the seam towards the facing. With the right side up, understitch close to the seam line and turn the facing to the inside. Tack the facings down at the shoulder seam and at the centre back.

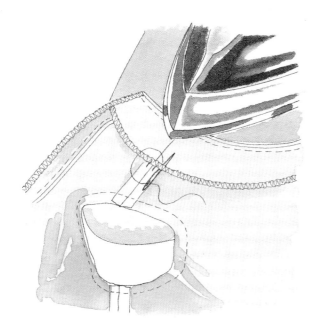

Combined facing

1 Fuse any necessary interfacings to the facings and join at the underarms only. Finish the edges of the facing as desired.

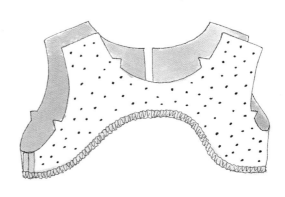

Pin a narrow tuck in the front and back shoulders of the garment; when released this will ensure that the facing seams do not show.

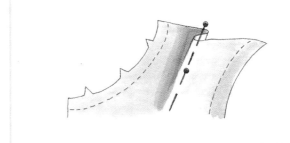

2 Pin the facing to the garment around the armholes and the front and back neckline. **NB The shoulder seams of the garment and the facings have not yet been joined.** Start and end stitching about 1 cm (⅜ in) away from shoulder edges. Trim, grade and clip the seam allowances.

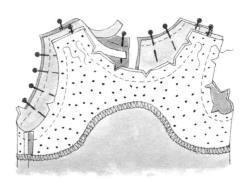

3 With the wrong side up, lightly press the seam allowances towards the facing. Turn the facing to the inside and, with the facing side up, understitch close to the seam line where possible. Press.

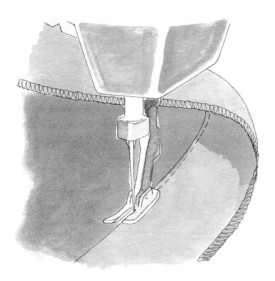

4 Release the tucks at the shoulders. With the neck and armhole seam allowances folded back and the facing folded out of the way, stitch the shoulder seams of the garment. Press the seams, first flat and then open, and push through the opening.

5 Trim the facing seam allowances to 6 mm (¼ in), turn under and then slipstitch by hand. Tack the facings down or 'stitch in the ditch' at all the strategic seams.

Bias facing

This facing is often used on sheer or bulky fabric instead of the conventional facing. It is cut on the bias to facilitate the curvature of the neck and is steamed into shape. The finished width ranges from 1 cm (⅜ in) to 2.5 cm (1 in).

1 Cut the bias strip twice the finished width plus twice the seam allowance. The length required must equal the total length of the neck seam line, from centre back to centre back, plus 5 cm (2 in) for seams and ease.

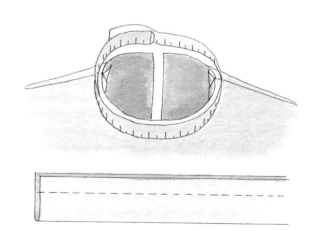

2 Fold in half lengthwise with wrong sides facing and then press flat, curving the strip with steam to match the curve of the neckline.

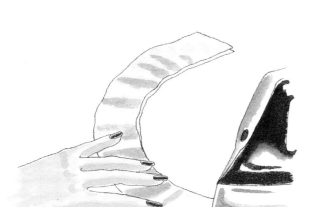

3 Pin the bias strip to the right side of the neckline, aligning the raw edges, and stitch. Press towards the bias strip, trim, grade and clip the seam allowances. Understitch close to the seam and turn the facing to the inside of the garment.

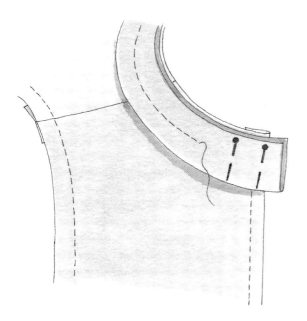

4 The edge of the bias facing may be slipstitched by hand or topstitched by machine. Two rows of topstitching are an attractive alternative.

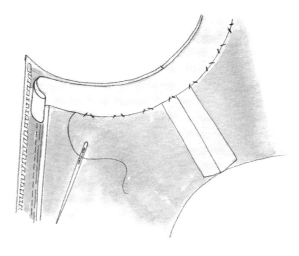

Piped (corded) facing

A piped neckline requires a facing to finish off the neck, with covered piping cord inserted between the garment and the facing. The same procedure applies for lace trims and other edgings, although the use of the zip foot is not applicable here.

1 Using a zip foot, attach the covered piping to the neckline, as instructed for the bias facing. Cut the cord flush with the centre back, trim the binding ends and fold in to align with the cord.

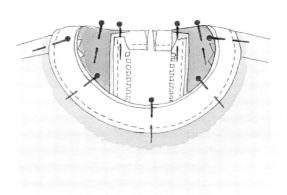

2 Place facing on top of the covered piping and
pin in position. Stitch, still using the zip foot.

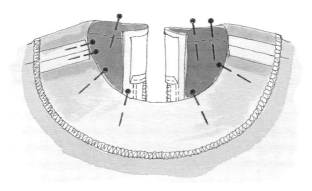

3 Press and trim, as previously instructed.
Understitch with the zip foot. Turn the facing
to the inside and tack down.

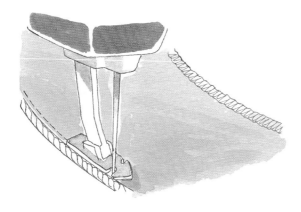

4 Slipstitch the ends of the cord closed for thin
piping cord; if a heavy piping cord has been
used, attach snap fasteners over the open ends.

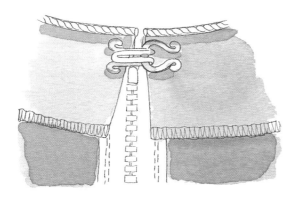

Ribbed bands

Whether interlocked or ribbed, knitted bands are a
suitable neckline finish for both knitted and woven
garments. However, because of its stretching
abilities, ribbing is preferable. Be sure to choose a
ribbing that is able to recover, i.e. to return to its
original shape after being stretched. Ribbing that
contains a certain percentage of lycra (elastic thread)
will retain its shape for a longer period. There are
two methods of attaching ribbed bands: the tubular
and the flat method.

ESTIMATING THE CUT SIZE
The finished width of a crewneck should be 2.5 cm
(1 in) to 3.2 cm (1¼ in); mock turtlenecks are 5 cm
(2 in); turtlenecks are 10 cm (4 in); and polo necks
are 15 cm (6 in) to 18 cm (7 in). Establish the
finished width desired and cut the ribbing to twice
this width plus 12 mm (½ in) for seam allowances.
To estimate the cut length of the neckband, measure
the neck seam line all round. Stand the tape
measure up on its side to determine this length
accurately. Cut the ribbing two-thirds the measured
length plus 12 mm (½ in) for seam allowances.

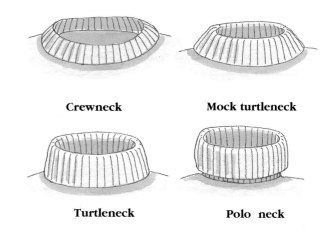

Crewneck   **Mock turtleneck**

Turtleneck   **Polo neck**

Tubular method

1 Join the ribbing ends using 6 mm (¼ in) seams. Fold in half lengthwise with wrong sides facing and divide into fourths. Mark with pins. Place a pin at the centre front and divide the neck into fourths from that point. Mark with pins.

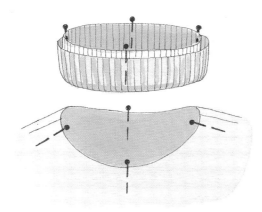

2 Match the pin markers of the ribbing to those of the neck, placing the seam at the left shoulder. **NB Placing the seam at the centre back looks unprofessional and is seldom, if ever, done in the commercial trade.**

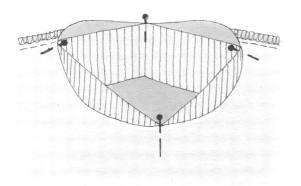

3 With the ribbing on top, stitch a 6 mm (¼ in) seam using an overedge stretch stitch, narrow zigzag or overlock. Stretch the ribbing to fit the garment neck between the pins. Press the seam towards the garment.

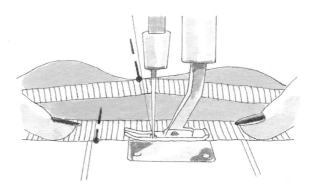

4 For a professional finish, bind the back neck, from shoulder to shoulder, encasing the seam allowance in the binding.

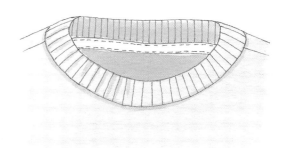

Flat method

1 Fold the ribbing in half lengthwise with wrong sides facing and divide into fourths. Mark with pins. **NB Only the right shoulder seam of the garment should be stitched closed at this point.** Divide the neck into fourths and mark with pins.

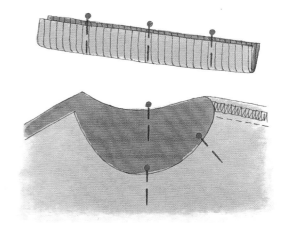

2 Match the pin markers of the ribbing and the neck and stitch as instructed for tubular method. Press the seam towards the garment.

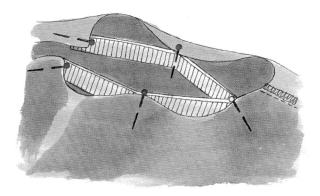

3 Stitch the open shoulder seam, taking care to match the ribbing ends and seams. Backstitch to secure the seam. The back neck seam may also be bound as for the tubular method.

'Quality distinguishes style from fashion.'

Giorgio Armani

Collars

Regardless of its style, a collar requires careful handling in every stage of construction to retain its quality appearance. The cutting of a collar also plays an important role: depending on the fabric, some under collars are cut on the bias grain and top collars on the straight grain or vica versa; interfacing is generally applied to the under collar, helping to define and support the collar's shape. There are, however, exceptions to these rules. Selecting the correct interfacing for the fabric used is imperative. First test the interfacing on a piece of scrap. For true professionalism, the top collar should be cut 3 mm (⅛ in) larger all round the outer edges. This will prevent the seams from showing when the collar is completed. Refer to Corners on page 39 before embarking on your collar construction. This is another aspect that requires special attention.

There are a few basic collar types which are all constructed in a slightly different way: the flat or Peter Pan collar, the convertible or notched revers collar, the shawl collar and the two-piece shirt collar. The notched revers collar on a shirt and on a jacket are also made in a slightly different way, mainly due to the variance in the weight of the fabric.

Flat collar

This collar is the simplest to construct but it does require a facing or binding on the inner edge. The Peter Pan and the sailor collar fall into this category.

This flat collar is slightly flared to soften the neckline.

1 Fuse the under collar with the appropriate interfacing and, with right sides facing, stitch top and under collars together around the outer edges.

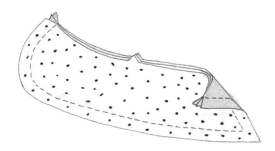

2 Trim, grade and notch the seam allowances. First press the seams open, then press the seam allowances towards the under collar. Understitch close to the seam line with the right sides facing.

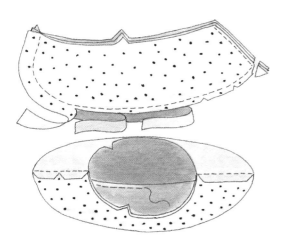

3 Turn right side out, push out the corners (refer to Corners on page 39) and, using slightly moist fingertips, work the outer seam line towards the under collar. Press with a pressing cloth and topstitch if desired.

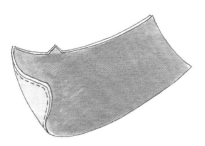

4 Staystitch the neckline before attaching the collar. Position the collar on the neckline, with the top collar facing up, align the appropriate notches and pin. Place the facing, with the right side down, on top of the collar, then match the notches and re-pin.

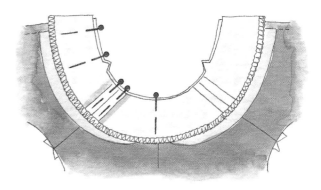

5 Stitch and finish referring to Piped (corded) facing on page 97.

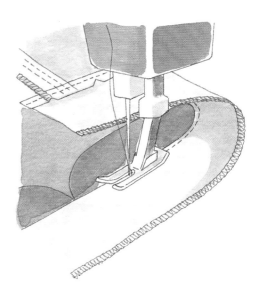

Notched shirt collar

This type of collar is also called a rolled collar as it can be worn open or closed. The roll is formed when the collar is curved around the neck, because the shape of the neckline edge of the collar is opposite to that of the neckline itself.

Lace has been used to highlight this notched shirt collar

1 Fuse the under collar with the appropriate interfacing and, with the right sides facing, stitch the top collar to the under collar around the outer edges.

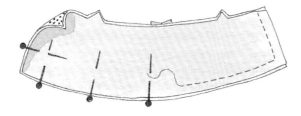

2 Trim, grade and notch the seam allowances, tapering at the corners. Press the seams flat and then open. Try not to press a crease into the collar. Understitch, close to the seam line where possible.

Turn to the right side, pull out the corners (refer to page 39) and, with slightly moistened fingertips, work the seam to the underside. Press. Topstitch at this stage if required.

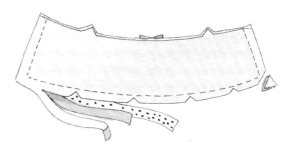

3 Clip the seam allowance of the top collar, at both the shoulder seams, to the seam line. Fold the seam allowance between these two notches under and press.

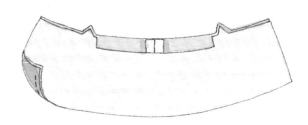

4 Fuse the front facing with the same interfacing as that used for the collar. Overlock or finish the edges as desired.

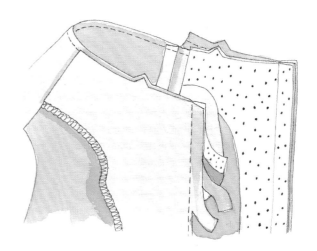

5 With the under collar facing the right side of the garment, position the collar on the neckline, matching all appropriate notches. Be sure to keep the folded back section of the top collar out if the way. Pin along the seam line.

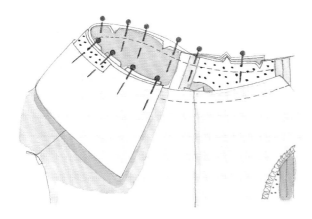

6 Turn the facing back on the fold or seam line (whichever is applicable) so that the right sides face. Match and pin the facing to the garment and the collar, clipping the facing seam allowance if necessary. The facing ends can either be folded back or just overlocked.

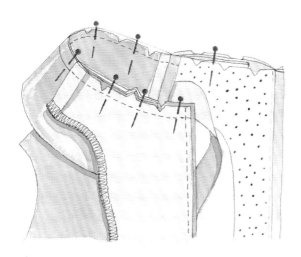

7 With the top collar facing up, carefully stitch from edge to edge along the seam line, taking special care not to catch the seam allowance at the back of the top collar. Press the back neck seams up towards the collar and the facing seams down towards the facing.

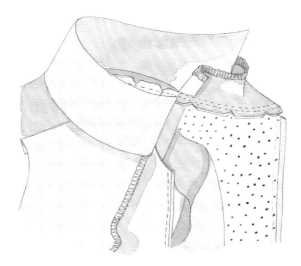

8 Turn the facing to the right side, pulling out the corners. Machine edgestitch or slipstitch the back seam of the top collar by hand. Tack the facing down at the shoulders or 'stitch in the ditch'. Press the collar and facing using a pressing cloth.

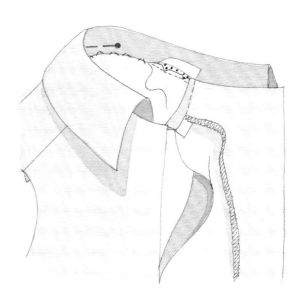

Notched jacket collar

The construction of a jacket collar varies slightly from that of a shirt collar, mainly due to the difference in the weight of the fabric. A crisp, flat, even notch is the hallmark of fine tailoring. The key to this detail is the clever combination of stitching and pressing, as well as careful trimming of the enclosed seam allowances to reduce bulk.

A classic notched jacket collar

'Clothes should feel wonderful to touch.'

Donna Karan

1 Fuse the necessary collars and facings with the appropriate interfacing. Join the shoulder seams of the facing and then staystitch the neck seam line on the jacket and the facing. Clip the seam allowances where necessary.

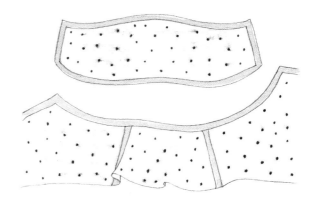

2 Match the notches of the under collar to the garment, pin in place and stitch, starting and ending at the lapel notches. Clip to these notches, press the seam open and trim the excess seam allowance to 6 mm (¼ in) to reduce bulk.

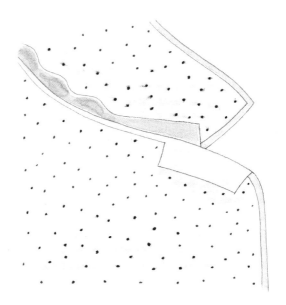

3 Repeat this procedure when attaching the top
collar to the facing. Trim the seam allowances
to 1 cm (⅜ in), slightly wider than those of the
undercollar, and press as before.

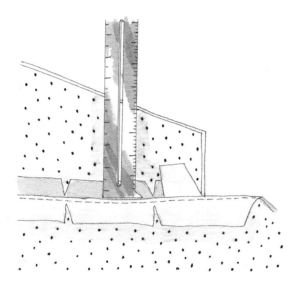

4 Pin the top collar/facing section to the under
collar/jacket section. Pin through the seams at
the collar notches, making sure that the seams line
up precisely. Trim the excess fabric of the collar
seam allowance to the stitching line on the top
and under collar.

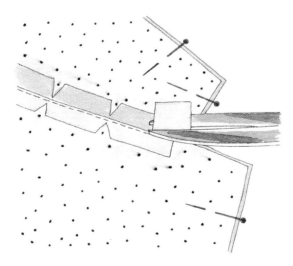

5 Stitch the seam, starting at the bottom of the
jacket edge. Take one or two short diagonal
stitches across the lapel point. Stitch from the lapel
point to the collar point, holding the seam straight
to ensure that the notches match on both sides of
the jacket collar. Finish stitching the seam, using
the same technique on the other side.

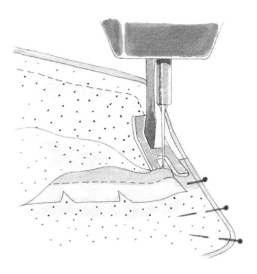

6 Press the seams open using the tip of the iron.
Diagonally trim the corners close to the
stitching. Trim the seam allowances of the under
collar/jacket to 6 mm (¼ in) and those of the top
collar/facing to 1 cm (⅜ in), continuing to the lapel
roll line notch. Clip this notch and continue
trimming the seam allowances: the jacket front to
1 cm (⅜ in) and the facing to 6 mm (¼ in). Press
the seam open and turn to the right side.

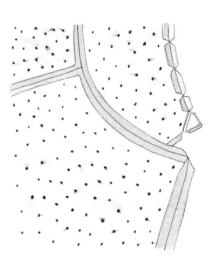

7 Stitch the top and under collar seams together. If the seams do not line up exactly because of the bulk of the fabric, tack the seams where they meet.

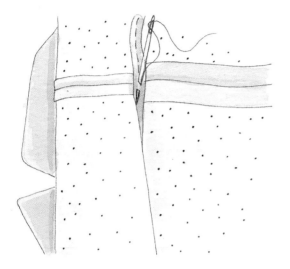

8 Press the collar and lapels from the underside. Roll the seam towards the underside of the collar and lapels, stopping about 2.5 cm (1 in) from the end of the roll line. Press and pound the edges with a tailor's clapper (block of wood) to create a crisp edge. Press the jacket front below the roll line from the inside so that the seams roll towards the jacket facing.

9 Topstitch on the right side of the jacket, starting at the one lower edge. Stop at the roll line and pull the threads through to the facing side, burying the ends between the facing and the garment.

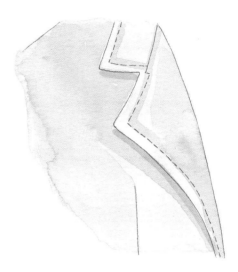

10 Continue on the right side of the lapel, overlapping the first two stitches at the start. At the collar notch, pivot and then stitch up to the notch edge. Pivot and 'stitch in the ditch' to the topstitching line of the collar. Pivot and stitch around the collar to the other notch. Repeat at the second notch, breaking the topstitching at the roll line on the other side. Pull the threads through as before and continue stitching on the jacket side to the lower edge.

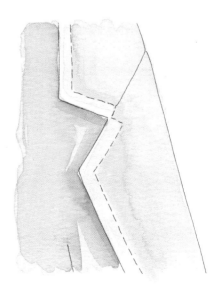

RIGHT: A double-breasted jacket with notched collar

Shawl collar

There is no distinction between the collar and lapels of a shawl collar. It is shaped in a continuous line with a centre back seam and is, therefore, easier to sew than a notched collar. When constructing a shawl collar on a jacket, be sure to press the seams open and grade the trimming of seam allowances, referring to the notched jacket collar (*see* page 104).

A classic shawl collar

1 Fuse the facing/top collar lapel with the appropriate interfacing. Stitch centre back seams, with right sides facing. Trim and press seam open.

2 Staystitch the back neck seam line, reinforcing the corners. Clip into the corners, then pin and stitch the back neck facing in place. Clip the seam allowances, press flat, trim to about 6 mm (¼ in) and press open.

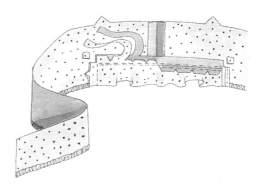

3 With right sides facing, match the under collar notches to the garment notches at the neckline. Pin in place and stitch. Clip the seam allowances and press the seam open.

4 With the right sides together, match and pin the collar/lapel/facing to the under collar, then stitch each side from the centre back down to the bottom edge. Clip at the end of the roll line. Press the seam flat.

5 Grade the seam allowance above the roll line notch, making the collar/lapel/facing unit the widest, and also below the roll line notch, making the garment seam allowance the widest. Clip and notch the seam and press open. Press the seam above the roll line notch towards the under collar, and below that point towards the facing.

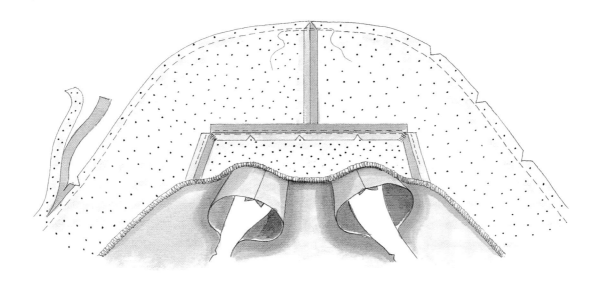

6 With the garment side up, understitch the outer edge of the collar and lapels; and with the facing side up, understitch the outer edge of the facing from the roll line to the hem.

7 With slightly moistened fingers, roll the seams under and press using a pressing cloth. Stitch the facing and the garment seam lines together and then secure the facings at the shoulder either by machine or by hand.

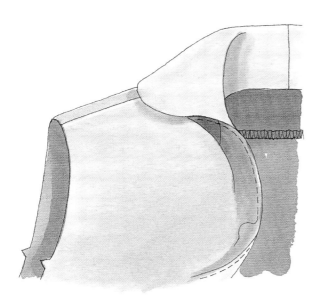

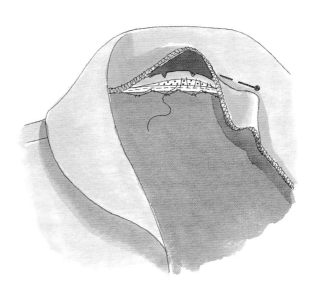

Two-piece shirt collar

This shirt collar consists of a separate collar and stand. It is commonly found in men's shirts but is also applicable for women's wear. Although the stand is usually separate, it may, however, be an extension of the collar unit and is constructed in the same way. As a rule, the interfacing is fused to the under collar, but for sheer and lightweight fabric, it should be fused to the top collar, preventing the seams from showing and ensuring a smooth finish. For the same reason, the collarstand always requires fusing on the outer side. If topstitching is required on the collar, do so before attaching it to the collarstand. This method eliminates all handstitching.

1 Fuse the collar and the stand with the appropriate interfacing. With the right sides facing, pin and stitch the top and under collars together, blunting the corners (refer to Corners on page 39). Press the seams flat and trim the edges and the corners.

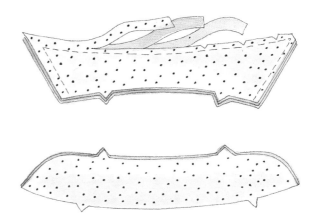

2 Press the seams open and then towards the under collar. Turn the collar to the right side and pull out the corners as instructed on page 39. Press on the underside and topstitch if required. Fold up the collarstand edge along its neck seam line and towards the wrong side. Press in position and then trim the seam allowance to 6 mm (¼ in).

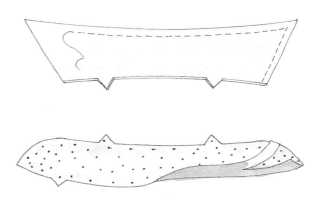

TOP LEFT AND LEFT: The separate collar stands are clearly visible in these two examples.

3 With right side of under collar facing right side of collarstand, match and pin together along the lower edge of the collar with the stands extending beyond the collar. Place collarstand facing on top, with right sides facing, align and pin together. Stitch along seam line, through all the layers, starting and ending 1 cm (⅜ in) from the edge, as illustrated.

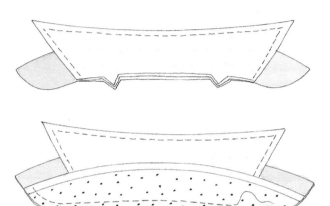

4 Press the seam flat, trim and grade the seams, making the seam of the facing wider, and notch and clip the curved seam allowances. Press the seams open using the tip of the iron. Turn to the right side and use a pressing cloth to press the seam, facing and stand down, away from the collar.

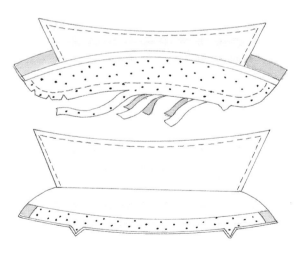

5 Staystitch the neckline of the garment and clip at intervals. With right side of the collarstand facing towards the wrong side of the garment, align and pin together along the neck seam. Stitch along the seam line, securing both ends.

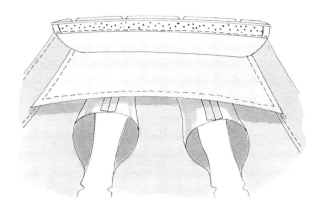

6 Trim, grade and clip the seam allowances where this is necessary. Press the seam open, then up towards the collar.

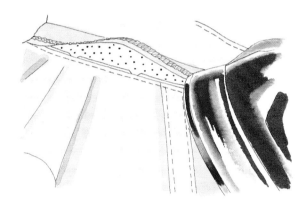

7 Align the collarstand edge with the neck seam line, pin in place and edgestitch carefully along all the edges of the collarstand, starting and ending on the upper edge at the centre back.

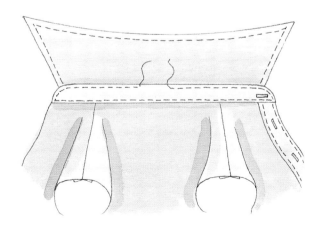

YOKES

The classic shirt yoke in both men's and ladies' clothing is fully lined so that all seams are enclosed. There are two techniques. The first one requires topstitching along the front seam. The back seam is usually also topstitched to balance with the front seam. The second method utilizes the pull-through technique and, even though it is machine stitched throughout, it requires no topstitching at all. This method is not difficult, but requires care when positioning the front shoulder seams. To prepare, first sew any tucks and gathers that might be required on the fronts or backs.

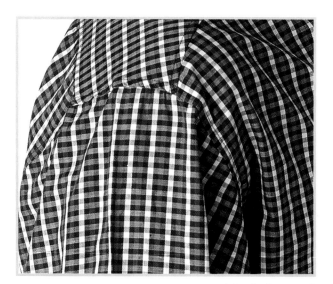
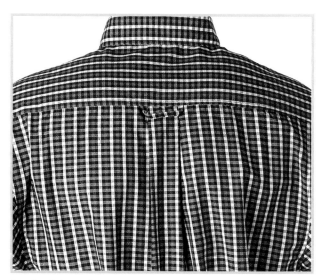

A typical example of a classic shirt yoke.

Topstitching method

1 With right sides together, pin the yoke to the shirt back. Pin the right side of the yoke facing to the wrong side of the shirt back. Stitch all three layers together using the given seam allowance. Press the yoke and facing upwards, away from the shirt, into the yoke's permanent position.

2 Topstitch the back yoke seam. Pin the right side of the yoke facing to the wrong side of the front shoulder seams. Stitch and press the seam upwards, towards the facing.

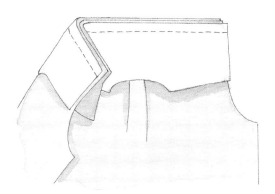

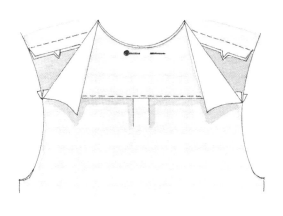

3 Press the seam allowance of the yoke shoulder seam under. Match the folded edge to the yoke facing seam line and topstitch. Staystitch the neck and shoulder edges together.

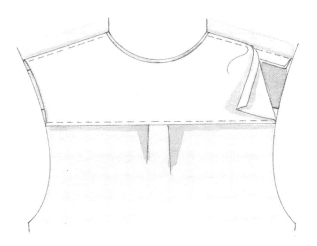

Pull-through technique

1 With right sides together, pin the yoke to the shirt back. Pin the right side of the yoke facing to the wrong side of the shirt back. Stitch all three layers together using the given seam allowance. Press the yoke and facing upwards, away from the shirt, into the yoke's permanent position.

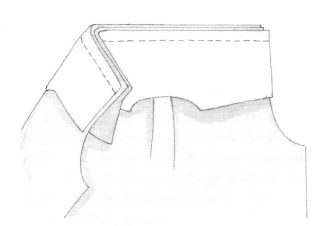

2 Do not topstitch the back yoke seam. Pin the right side of the yoke facing to the wrong side of the shirt fronts at the shoulder seams. Roll up the back and fronts together, starting at the hem. With right sides together, match the shoulder seams of the yoke and the shirt fronts. (The shirt will be between the yoke and the yoke facing.) Stitch the three layers of the yoke, shirt front and yoke facing together.

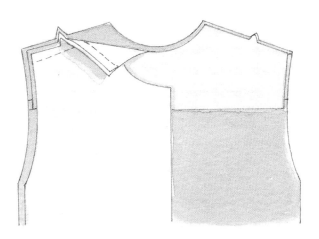

3 To complete, pull the whole shirt through the shoulder opening to the right side. Finally, press the front shoulder seams flat.

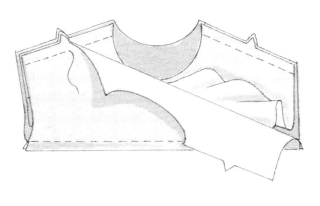

WAISTBANDS

A well-sewn and fitted waistband never stretches, wrinkles or folds over. Most waistbands need to be reinforced with the correct interfacing to prevent this. These interfacings are available in pre-cut widths, with or without perforated slots. The single row of perforated slots is off-centre, allowing the extra width for the inside of the waistband so that the edge can be caught as you stitch from the outside. The triple perforated slots allow both edges to be folded over.

In the early 1990s the traditional waistband was replaced with bias piping and this is still a popular finish today. Straight waistbands should not be wider than 5 cm (2 in) but contoured waistbands are wider and shaped to accommodate the difference in the girth between the waist and hips or the waist and rib cage. Stretch waistbands allow for comfort and ease and are made of either decorative elastic or elastic threaded through a fabric casing. A facing will provide a clean, smooth finish and does not extend above the waistline edge. This facing may be cut in self fabric, otherwise a grosgrain/petersham ribbon can be used.

Positioning

To enable the waistband of a garment to fit properly, it is important to find the exact placement of the seam on the body. To do this, tie a piece of string snugly enough around the waistline to hold the garment up. Adjust the garment to fit smoothly around the hips with the darts in the right position. For trousers, pull them up until they fit well in the crotch. Mark the waist seam line directly beneath the string, add on the seam allowance and then trim off the excess.

Straight waistband

1 Select the appropriate interfacing for your fabric and fuse the waistband. Overlock the inside edge if the selvedge has not been used and if slipstitching is not required.

2 Fold the waistband in half lengthwise, with right sides facing, and stitch across both ends. Trim the seam allowances to 6 mm (¼ in) and trim across the corners. Turn to the right side and press.

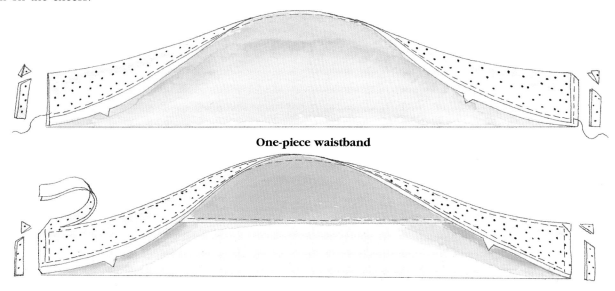

One-piece waistband

Two-piece waistband

3 Staystitch the garment waist seam line. With right sides together, pin the waistband to the garment edge, carefully matching all notches. Ensure that the left back edge is flush with the edge of the zip and the underlap is on the right back side.

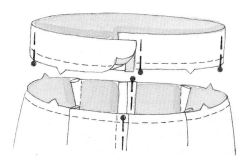

4 Stitch, easing the garment if necessary, but be sure not to allow any tucks to form. Press, grade, trim and clip the seam.

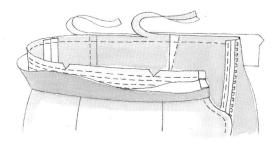

5 Turn to the right side and press the seam up towards the waistband. Fold up the seam allowance of the facing at the underlap and edgestitch the lower edge of the waistband, with right side up, so that the facing is automatically caught in the seam. Alternatively, if no edgestitching is required, 'stitch in the ditch' or fold up the seam allowance of the entire facing and slipstitch.

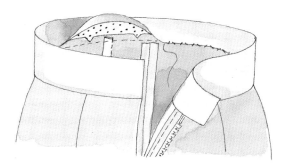

For a quick and easy method, follow steps 1 to 3 and then staystitch the waist seam line. Fold the outer seam allowance up and press flat. Encase the waistline in the waistband, aligning the folded edge with the staystitching of the waist. Pin in place and edgestitch or 'stitch in the ditch'.

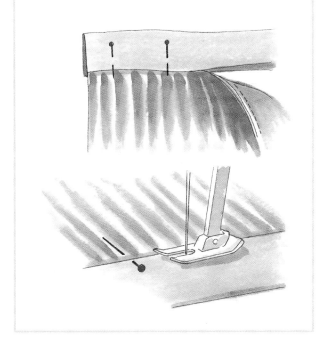

Grosgrain faced waistband

This facing reduces bulk and is particularly suitable on heavy fabrics. Fuse the waistband, as required. Attach the ribbon by lapping the edge of the ribbon over the right side of the waistband upper seam allowance. Pin in place and edgestitch the ribbon. Proceed as for the straight waistband.

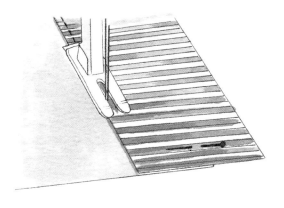

Contoured waistband

Waistbands that exceed 5 cm (2 in) in width need to be contoured to fit the curves of the body. Some trouser waistbands, although not necessarily wide, are also shaped for more comfort and a better fit. These have a centre back seam, which is cut slightly on the bias, allowing the centre front edges to be on the straight grain.

1 Fuse the waistband facing with the appropriate interfacing. Depending on the weight of the fabric used, the waistband itself might need fusing.

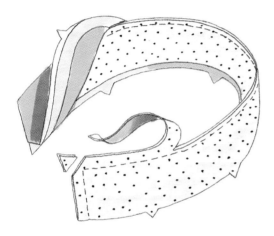

2 Join the facing to the waistband along the upper seam. Press, trim and grade the seam allowance as required. Continue, following the instructions given for the straight waistband.

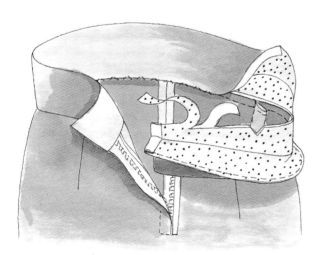

Bias piped waistband

Bias piping can be applied to any waistline that calls for a straight waistband. It is advisable to test a short bias piece of the required fabric to ascertain the amount of stretch it contains. Measure the relaxed state, then measure the stretched state. Deduct the difference from the waist measurement. The finished width may vary from 12 mm (½ in) to 1.5 cm (⅝ in). For a 12 mm (½ in) piping, cut a 6.5 cm (2 ½ in) strip; for a 1.5 cm (⅝ in) piping, cut a 7.5 cm (3 in) strip. Remember to add 2 cm (¾ in) to the length determined in order to allow for seams.

1 Fold the bias strip in half lengthwise, with the wrong sides together and the raw edges aligned. Press lightly.

2 With right sides facing, align the edges of the waistline and the bias strip, allowing each end to extend by 1 cm (⅜ in). Pin in place and stitch.

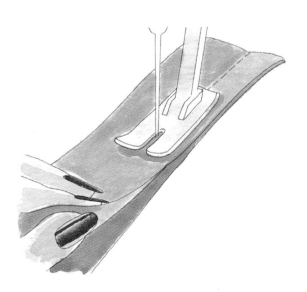

3 Press the seam allowance up towards the bias strip, using your finger. Fold the bias strip down towards the inside of the garment, so that the edge of the strip extends slightly beyond the waist seam line, and pin in place. 'Stitch in the ditch' on the right side of the garment.

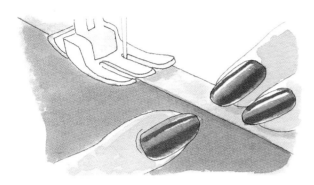

4 Using an awl, push the 1 cm (⅜ in) extensions at the zip inside the piping and slipstitch closed. Attach a hook and eye to the ends of the piping.

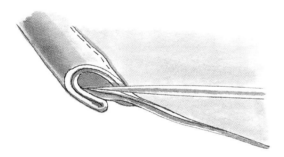

Faced waistline

Facings are applicable on skirts and trousers where no waistbands are required. They can either be made from self fabric, lining or grosgrain ribbon. The need for interfacing would depend on the weight of the fabric used. This finish is particularly suitable for hipsters.

1 Fuse the facing with the appropriate interfacing, if required. Join the side seams and finish the outer edge with overlocking or other suitable seam finish (refer to page 36).

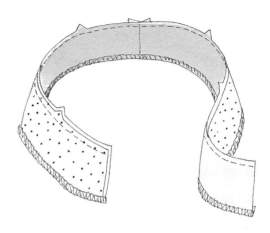

2 With right sides together, position the facing on the waistline of the garment, aligning any notches and pin in place. Be sure to tuck the ends of the facing under, towards the inside of the garment. To reinforce the waist, pin 6 mm (¼ in) cotton tape to the seam line. This will replace staystitching the garment.

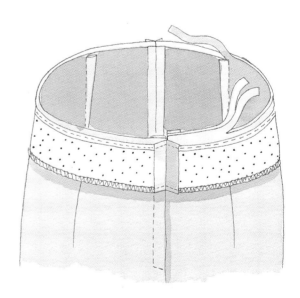

3 Stitch the seam and press flat. Trim, grade and clip the seams. Press the seams up towards the facing and then understitch close to the seam line, through all the layers. This will prevent the facing from rolling towards the outside of the garment.

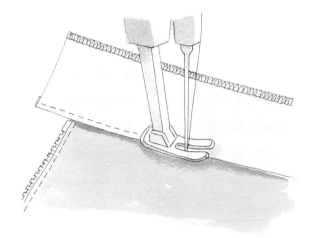

4 Turn the facing towards the inside and press along the waist edge. Tack the facing down at the seams and darts. Slipstitch the facing ends to the zip tape. Attach a hook and eye above the zip.

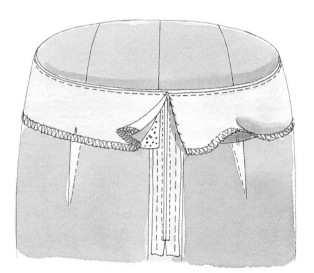

Grosgrain faced waistline

If curved grosgrain ribbon is not available, shape the ribbon accordingly by steaming it in order to shrink the waist edge and curve the outer edge. Staystitch the waist seam line, trim the seam allowance and lap the wrong side of the ribbon over the right side of the garment. Pin in position, folding the ends under towards the inside, and edgestitch the ribbon. Turn to the inside, press and tack down as for the faced waistline.

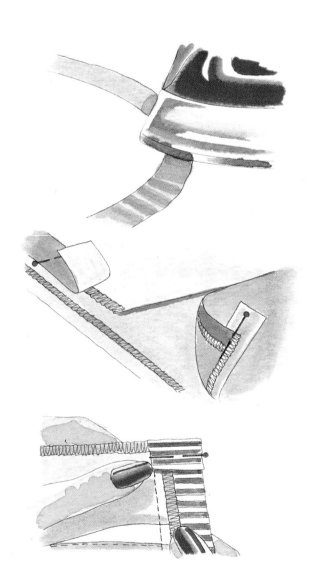

A straight waistband

An elasticated waistband

**The contrast topstitching highlights
the waistband, seams and pocket details.**

**This waistband is extended into the
basque and boned for support.**

Elasticated waistband

This finish is only suitable on garments without waist darts. For an inclusive waistband, extend the waist edge of the garment by twice the width of the elastic plus 1 cm (⅜ in). Alternatively, cut a separate waistband, twice the width of the elastic plus 2 cm (¾ in) for seams. The choice of elastic is important: select a firm quality that will not roll or fold over.

1 Measure the elastic snugly around the waistline, mark the meeting point and add 1 cm (⅜ in) for the overlap. Cut and join the elastic according to this measurement. Overlock the raw edge of the waistband and fold the casing towards the inside of the garment, according to the width of the elastic, plus 1 cm (⅜ in). Press a crease at the fold. Ensure that the seams of the garment are pressed open or flat. Slip the elastic over the wrong side of garment waistline and sandwich it inside the folded casing.

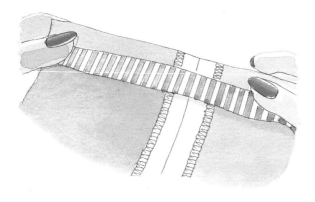

2 With wrong side up, stitch, keeping the casing to the right of the needle. The 1 cm (⅜ in) overlocked seam should be to the left of the needle.

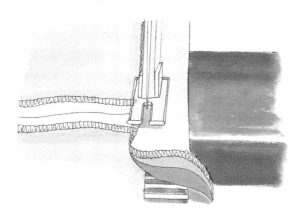

Using a zip foot when stitching the casing will allow you to sew close to the elastic. Be sure not to catch the elastic when doing so. Alternatively, the elastic may be zigzagged onto the fabric.

3 To prevent stitching onto the elastic, keep your index finger on the edge of the elastic closest to the edge of the casing. Continue until the fabric is gathered too much to sew any further. Stop with the needle down, lift the foot, pull the elastic towards you, and continue stitching to the end of the seam.

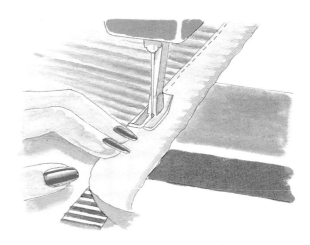

4 Distribute the gathers evenly by stretching the elastic to its fullest point. Steam the waistband slightly to shrink the elastic and flatten the gathers.

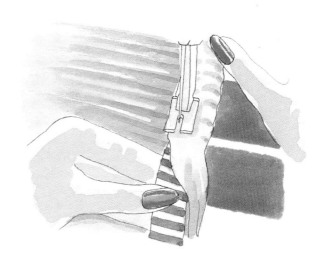

Decorative stretch waistbands

Decorative elastic is available in various weights and widths from about 2.5 cm (1 in) upwards. It may be woven, braided or shirred and obtainable in solid colours, plaids or stripes. The application of the elastic will be determined by the finish of the elastic edges.

1 Measure the elastic as previously instructed and then cut accordingly. Overlock the ends and, with the right sides together, stitch the seam. Press the seam open, turn back the top corners diagonally and whipstitch the seam allowances to the waistband. Staystitch the waistline seam of the garment and trim to 6 mm (¼ in).

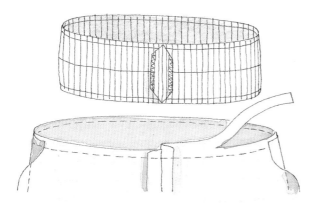

'The sweatshirt equates comfort, which is what modern clothes should be.'

Geoffrey Beene

2 Divide the garment and elastic into four equal parts and mark with pins. For elastic with both edges finished, lap the wrong side of the elastic onto the right side of the garment, placing the elastic seam at the centre back and matching the pins. For one unfinished edge, place the elastic inside the garment with right sides facing.

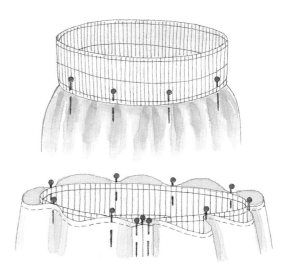

3 Zigzag close to the edge on the outside of the elastic, or sew along the indicated stitching line. Be sure to stretch the elastic carefully between the pins as you stitch to fit the garment. Steam the elastic and the gathers slightly.

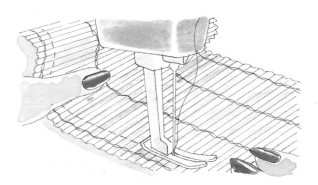

SLEEVES

There are three basic sleeve types: set-in, kimono and raglan. The set-in sleeve has a rounded head which must be eased to fit smoothly into the armhole; the kimono sleeve extends without seams from the front and back of the garment and may have rounded shoulder shaping and soft drapes under the arms; and the raglan has a slanted seam in the front and back with either a shaped shoulder seam or a dart at the shoulder. It is imperative to align all notches carefully in order to maintain a professional finish.

This basic set-in shirt sleeve is finished off with a contrasting cuff.

Set-in sleeve

The flat method of inserting a sleeve is by far the simplest. Using this technique, decorative topstitching and French seams can be applied with ease. It is also ideal for men's shirts and children's wear. Depending on the curve of the sleeve, the head needs to be manipulated carefully when it is eased into an armhole to avoid any puckers. This is aggravated when the sleeve and the armhole have been closed prior to being attached. The two-piece sleeve of a jacket, however, needs to be inserted into the closed armhole and very often requires adjusting according to the shape of the shoulder.

1 Join the shoulder seams of the garment, finish the edges and press the seams open. For a closed seam, press the seam towards the back.

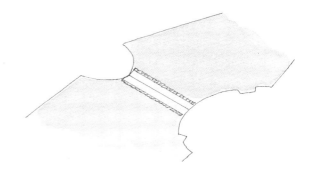

2 If required, easestitch the sleeve head between the notches and draw up the threads so that the notches fit those of the armhole. (This will also apply to a gathered crown.) Secure the ends and steam-press along the head to shrink out as much of the puckering as possible.

3 With the right sides facing, match and pin the sleeve to the armhole, aligning the notches. Stitch with the sleeve side up.

4 Trim the shoulder cross-seam allowances diagonally. If topstitching or any other decorative stitching is required around the armhole, overlock the seam edges or apply another appropriate finish. Press these seam allowances towards the garment and with right side up, stitch accordingly. If no topstitching is required, trim the seam to 6 mm (¼ in) and finish the edges. Press the seams towards the sleeve.

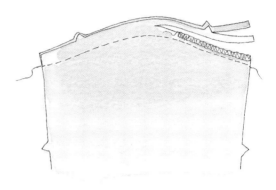

5 With the right sides facing, match and pin the underarm seams. Stitch one continuous seam from the hem of the garment to the hem of the sleeve. Diagonally trim the cross-seam allowances, then trim the seam allowances to 6 mm (¼ in) and finish the edges.

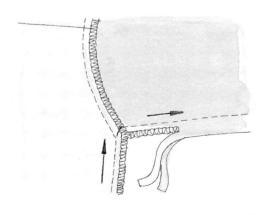

When overlocking, it is unnecessary to trim the seams prior to stitching. All overlockers have built-in blades that trim and stitch simultaneously.

Kimono sleeve

The kimono sleeve is cut as an extension of the bodice and, depending on the degree of the sleeve's shoulder slope and underarm curve, may be either loose or close fitting. Due to stress on the underarm, it is necessary to reinforce that section of the underarm with cotton tape. For added ease and comfort, a gusset may be inserted at the underarm.

1 Stitch the shoulder seams, finish the edges and press open, or towards the back if closed. With right sides facing, match and pin the front to the back. Centre and pin a 10 cm (4 in) piece of tape to the seam line at the curve of the underarm.

2 Stitch from the hem of the garment to the hem of the sleeve, attaching the tape, as pinned. Clip the seam allowances along the curve, taking care not to cut the tape. Trim and finish the seams and press open. Closed seams must face towards the back.

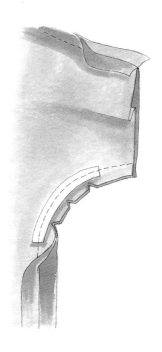

3 Alternatively, attach the tape after the seam is stitched and pressed open. First clip the seams and then attach the tape. This method is suitable for heavier fabrics as it is less bulky.

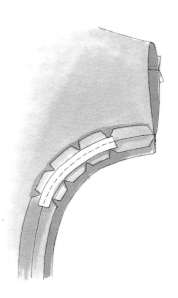

Raglan sleeve

This sleeve is popular because of its comfortable fit and simple construction. It may be cut on the straight or bias grain and may be one-piece, with a shoulder dart, or two-piece, with a shaped shoulder.

2 With right sides facing, match, pin and stitch the front armhole to the front sleeve. Repeat at the back. Trim and finish the edges and press the seams open, from the neck to the notches, or towards the sleeve if closed. If topstitching is required, press the seam towards the garment.

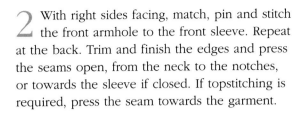

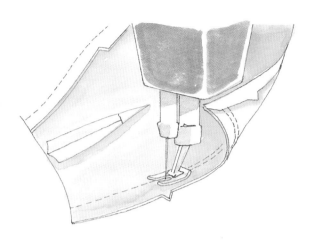

1 With right sides facing, match, pin and stitch the shoulder dart (for the one-piece) or the shoulder seam (for the two-piece). Press the seams flat. Clip, trim and finish the edges, and press the seams open, or towards the back if closed.

3 With right sides facing, match and pin the underarm seams. Stitch from the hem of the garment to the hem of the sleeve. Trim the cross-seams diagonally and trim and finish the seams. Press the seams open, or towards the back if closed.

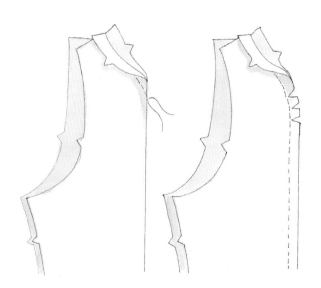

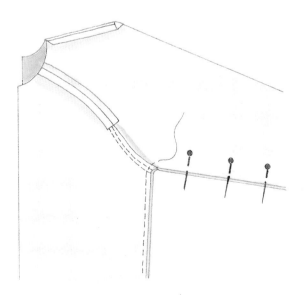

Gussets

A gusset is a diamond-shaped piece of fabric that is inserted into an opening at the underarm of a kimono sleeve. It provides ease and flexibility and allows a closer fit to the body.

The two-piece gusset is easier to insert. Each half can be attached to the corresponding half of the sleeve prior to joining the underarm seams.

Because it receives the maximum amount of strain, the gusset should always be cut on the bias.

Half the gusset can be seen on this sleeve

1 Cut a 5 cm (2 in) square of fabric or lining on the bias to reinforce the point of the slashed opening. On the right side of the garment, centre the patch over the slash point, pin and tack in position.

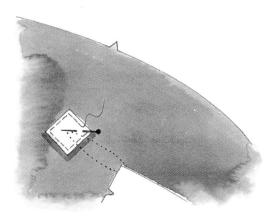

2 Staystitch close to the stitching line. Stitch from the underarm to the point, pivot, take one stitch across, pivot again and stitch down the other side.

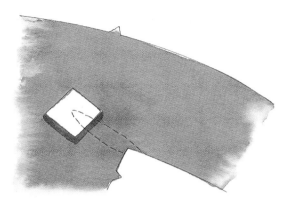

3 Press the area flat and then slash through the centre of the opening, cutting through the patch as well. Turn to the wrong side and press lightly.

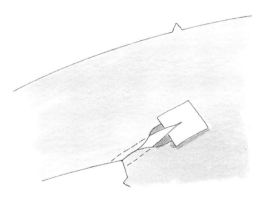

4 With right sides together, pin and stitch the garment and sleeve seams repectively. Trim and finish the edges and press the seams open.

5 Position the gusset over the slashed opening, aligning the corresponding notches. Pin and stitch with the garment side up. At each corner, pivot, take one stitch across the point, pivot again and continue to the next corner.

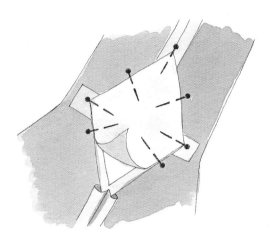

6 Press seams towards garment, trim and finish the edges. For extra strength, the gusset may be edgestitched close to the seam line on the outside.

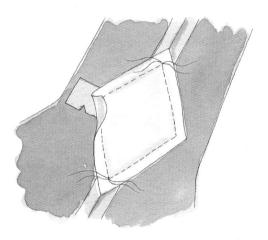

Sleeve finishes

The finish applied to the sleeve hem requires careful attention. There are various methods applicable, and these can easily be followed by referring to the appropriate instructions discussed on pages 60–66. The sleeve may be hemmed or faced; it may have an elastic casing or a ribbed cuff as on a sweatshirt; or it may be finished off with a shirt cuff. Be sure that the finish you select is compatible with garment.

Elastic casing

This finish is suitable on most fabrics and is very practical for children's wear, blouses and sportswear. A casing is created at the hem through which elastic is threaded. The sleeve is cut longer to allow a gathered flounce to fall slightly over the casing.

1 Allow enough casing width below hemline to equal the width of the elastic plus 1 cm (⅜ in). Turn 3 mm (⅛ in) to the wrong side at the edge and press. Turn casing towards the inside along marked hemline and pin in position. Stitch, as illustrated, leaving a small opening through which to thread the elastic. Stitch another row close to the folded edge.

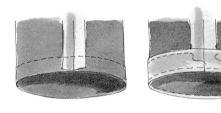

2 Measure elastic snugly around wrist and add 1 cm (⅜ in) for the overlap. Cut and, using a bodkin or safety pin, thread elastic through casing. Be sure not to twist the elastic. Overlap the ends and stitch, as illustrated. Edgestitch the opening.

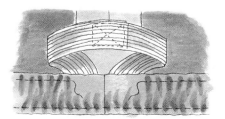

Ribbed cuff

These knitted bands are a popular choice to finish the sleeves of sweatshirts, T-shirts, pyjamas and children's wear. They are most suitable on knitted fabrics that stretch and also on loose-fitting sleeves where woven fabric has been used.

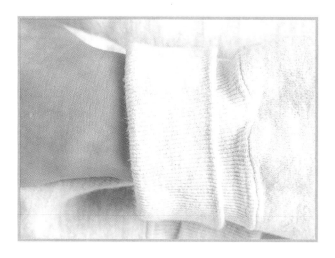

1 Establish the width of the finished cuff and cut twice the width plus 12 mm (½ in) for seams. Measure the length snugly around the wrist and add 12 mm (½ in) for seams.

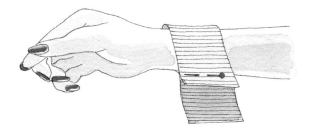

2 With right sides facing and raw edges together, fold cuff in half widthwise and stitch the seam.

3 With wrong sides facing, fold the cuff in half lengthwise and divide into four equal parts. Mark with pins. Divide the sleeve into four equal parts at the hem and pin.

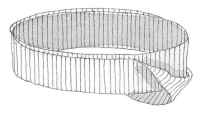

4 With the right sides together, pin the cuff to the sleeve, matching the seams and aligning the pins. With the cuff side up, stitch the cuff to the sleeve, stretching the cuff to lie flat against the edge of the sleeve.

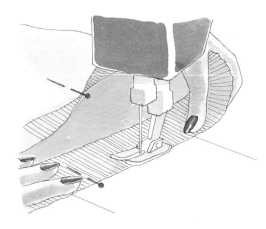

5 Overlock the edges and then press the seam towards the sleeve.

Shirt cuff

Most shirt cuffs are cut in one piece and require interfacing to maintain a crisp look. The entire cuff may be fused, providing the weight of the interfacing is compatible with that of the fabric. In many ways, sewing cuffs is similar to sewing collars.

Wide cuff with decorative buttons

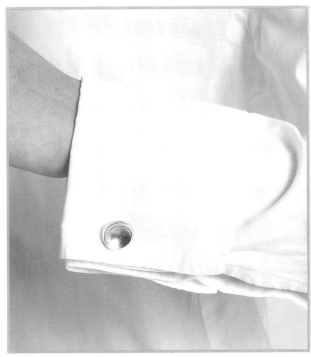

Turned back cuff fastened with cuff links

1 Select the appropriate interfacing and fuse the cuffs. Press the seam allowance of the cuff up towards the fold line.

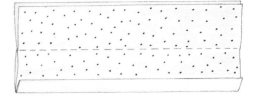

2 With right sides facing, fold the cuff in half lengthwise and stitch the ends. Press the seam flat. Trim the seam allowances, tapering the corners. Turn to the right side and pull out the corners. Roll the facing edges slightly under and press.

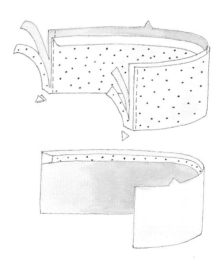

3 Staystitch any tucks required at the sleeve hem; or easestitch and draw up the necessary fullness, if required. Select the appropriate placket (*see* page 69) and finish the slit edge.

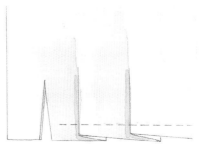

4 Pin the right side of the cuff facing to the wrong side of the sleeve, keeping the cuff ends flush with the underlap and overlap edges of the placket. Be sure to draw up any remaining excess to the sleeve. Distribute any gathers evenly.

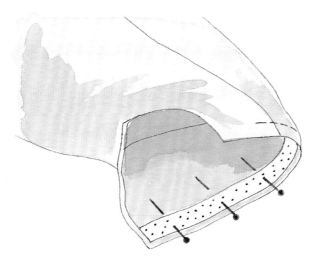

5 Stitch, securing the threads at each end. Press the seam flat, trim the cross-seam allowances and then grade the seams so that the widest seam is next to the cuff.

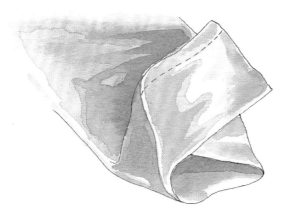

6 Pull the cuff down and press the seam allowances towards the cuff. Align the folded edge of the cuff just over the stitching line on the right side of the sleeve. Pin in position and edge-stitch. Continue this edgestitching around the entire cuff, if desired. Secure the threads and press.

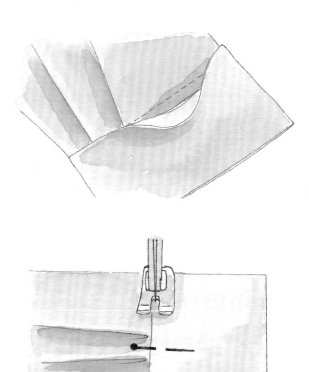

7 If a plain lapped cuff is required without topstitching, attach the cuff to the outside of the sleeve, with the right sides facing. Turn to the inside and slipstitch the cuff facing.

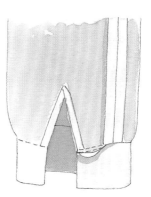

POCKETS

Pockets may be decorative, where position, size and shape can be just about anything, but should remain flattering; or they may be functional, and should fall comfortably within the hand's reach. There are generally two types of pockets: the patch pocket and the inside pocket. Patch pockets are stitched on top of the garment and can be virtually any shape and decorated with various trimmings. The inside pocket may be sewn into the opening of a seam; the front curved pocket is attached at the waist and side seam; and the slashed pocket is finished with a welt or flap.

Patch pockets

These pockets are finished on all sides and then attached to the garment. They may be lined or unlined, single or in pairs. Ensure that the paired pockets are exactly the same size and shape, and also that the positioning marks are equidistant. Bias cut pockets should be fully fused to avoid stretching out, whereas pockets cut on the straight grain only need fusing on the facing. If a separate pocket flap is required, be sure to fuse it as well. This flap should be positioned about 1.5 cm (⅝ in) above the top of the pocket.

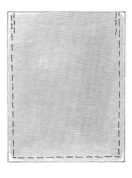

Use a cardboard template, cut to the finished size of the pocket, to guide stitching and pressing.

LEFT: Patch pockets can enhance a plain shirt whilst the inside pockets on these classic trousers are functional.

Unlined patch pockets

1 Fuse the pocket facing with the appropriate interfacing and overlock the edge of the facing. Fold the facing to the right side along the fold line, i.e. the edge of the interfacing, and stitch each side on the seam line, as illustrated.

2 For rounded corners, easestitch at each corner, slightly to the outside of the seam line. For squared corners, mitre as instructed on page 40.

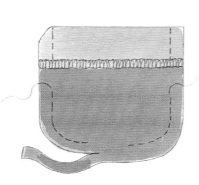

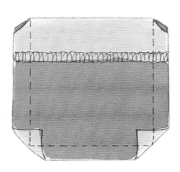

3 Trim the top corners diagonally, turn to the right side and pull out the corners. Press the top edge. Draw up the easestitching and notch out any excess fabric. Press the pocket seam allowances flat. Pin the pocket onto the garment, carefully matching the markings, and edgestitch in place.

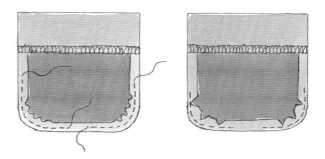

Be sure to reinforce the top corners of the pocket. Small identical triangles or rectangles, backstitching or bartacking are all methods suitable for this task.

Lined patch pockets

1 Fuse the pocket facing with the appropriate interfacing. With the right sides facing, pin and stitch the lining to the facing, leaving a small opening in the centre of the seam for turning, Press the seam towards the lining.

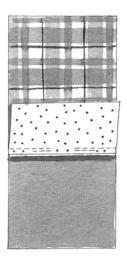

2 With right sides together, match the bottom edges of the lining and the pocket, pin and stitch around the edges. Press flat. Trim and grade the seam allowances. Trim the corners and notch out the rounded corners.

Cut the lining of the pocket 3 mm (¹/₈ in) smaller all round. This will prevent the seams from showing when the pocket is turned.

3 Carefully turn the pocket to the right side through the opening in the facing. Roll the seam to the underside and press flat. The opening can be slipstitched, but it is not essential to do so. Pin the pocket onto the garment, carefully matching the markings, and edgestitch in place.

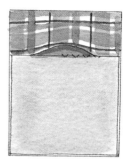

Inside pockets

These pockets are generally concealed in the side seams or hidden behind a welt or flap. The front-hip pockets must be included in any alterations to the waist or hip. To eliminate unnecessary bulk, the pocket facing may be cut in lining, but the pocket must be cut in self fabric. It is advisable to reinforce the pocket opening with tape or a strip of inter-facing to prevent it from stretching out.

In-seam pocket

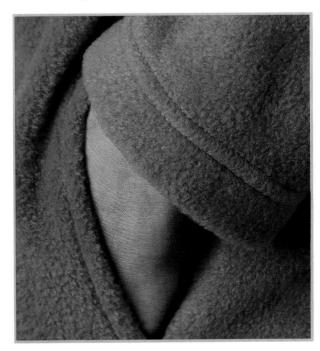

1 Cut a piece of tape about 5 cm (2 in) longer than the opening of the pocket. Reinforce the front of the garment along the pocket opening by positioning the piece of tape on the wrong side of the pocket seam line. Centre the tape next to the pocket opening marks. Stitch 3 mm (⅛ in) from the edge nearest the seam line, as illustrated.

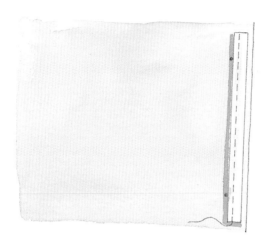

2 With right sides facing, pin and stitch the pocket facing to the garment, if it has not been cut all-in-one with the garment. Press the seam flat, trim the seam as illustrated, and then overlock the edges. Turn the pocket away from the garment and press the seam towards the garment.

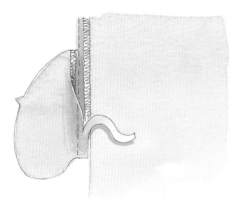

3 Hand tack the pocket opening. With the right sides together, match and pin the front of the garment to the back. Stitch around the pocket and the side seams. Reinforce the corners of the pocket opening by backstitching.

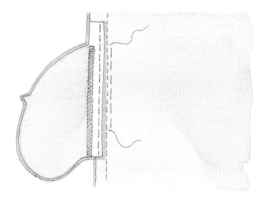

4 Press the seam flat to embed the stitches and then clip the seam allowance of the back section of the garment at the corners. Press open the garment seam above and below the pocket. Overlock the edges, catching in the garment front seam allowance at the top and bottom. Press the pocket towards the garment front and remove the tacking at the opening.

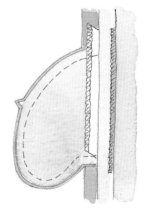
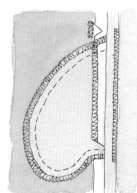

Front-hip pocket

1 Fuse the garment at the shaped edge of the pocket with a suitable interfacing cut 5 cm (2 in) wide and shaped to fit.

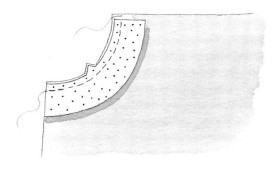

2 With right sides facing, pin and stitch the pocket facing to the garment along the opening edge of the pocket. Press flat, then trim and grade the seam, leaving the garment seam the widest. Clip or notch out the curves.

3 Press the seam open to flatten, then press both seams towards the facing. Understitch the facing close to the seam line, through all the layers. Turn the facing towards the inside and press. If any topstitching is required, do so at this stage.

4 With right sides together, pin and stitch the pocket to the facing. Press and overlock the edges. Attach the back of the garment to the front along the side seams, catching the side edges of the pockets in the seams.

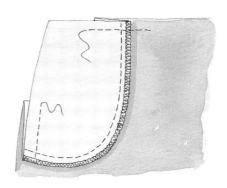

To flatten the tummy, extend the pocket to the fly-front seam. This will also prevent the pocket opening from pulling at the side seam.

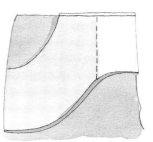

Single welt pocket

3 With right sides facing and raw edges together, pin and stitch the welt to the pocket facing. With the wrong side of the garment facing the right side of the pocket facing, slide the welt through the window frame, aligning the raw edges of the welt/facing seam with the bottom edge of the window frame.

1 Fuse the welt and a narrow strip at the pocket opening, using the appropriate interfacing. Fold the welt in half lengthwise, with right sides facing, and pin and stitch the ends. Trim the seams and the corners and turn to the right side. Press.

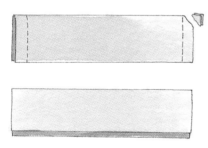

4 Pin and stitch across the bottom edge of the window frame, through all the layers, with the garment on top and the pocket facing underneath. Be sure not to stitch beyond the ends of the frame. In the same manner, pin and stitch the pocket to the top edge of the window frame.

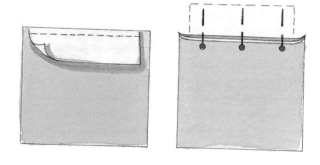

2 Mark the welt's window frame, as indicated on your pattern, as well as the centre line. Cut along this centre line, and then into each corner, stopping just short of the stitching.

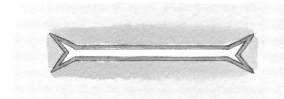

5 Place the garment right side up on the machine and flip back enough garment to expose the triangular ends. Stitch back and forth across the triangle and stitch one continuous seam, joining the pocket facing to the pocket. Repeat the reinforcement to the triangle on the other side. Overlock the pocket edges. Reinforce the ends of the welts with edgestitching or slipstitch by hand.

6 If the welt is the same width as the window frame, the window frame may be topstitched, for a sporty look. Press the seams of the window frame back and, with right side up, edgestitch across the bottom edge of the frame. Stitch the triangles and the pocket bag, as previously instructed, and then edgestitch the three remaining sides of the window frame on the right side. Bartack the sides of the welt to strengthen the stress points.

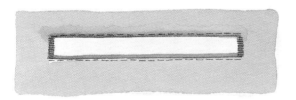

'There is no fashion without personal style.'

Zoran

Double welt or bound pocket

1 Follow the instructions given on pages 78–79 for the one-piece folded bound buttonhole from step 1 to step 4, positioning the pocket and facing on top of the strip, with the opening ends meeting at the centre line, as illustrated.

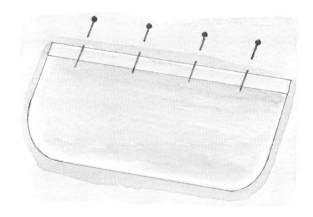

2 Now continue through to step 7 on page 79, pushing the welts and the pocket pieces through the opening.

3 Follow step 5 for the single welt pocket above left. If a pocket flap is required as well, sandwich the finished flap between the strip and the pocket before stitching.

CONSTRUCTION

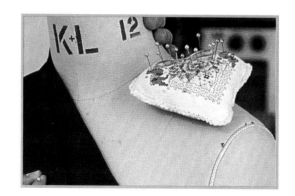

A perfect fit is achieved by assembling the separate pieces of a garment in the proper order and carefully checking that each piece fits the body before proceeding to the next step. Darts, tucks, collars and cuffs and other finishes need to be completed before attaching them in their required positions and only then is the garment ready to be assembled. It is easier to stitch a zip into a flat, unclosed piece of fabric rather than trying to reach into the garment in order to attach it. To prevent any delicate beads from getting crushed, it is advisable to bead the garment after you have completed it but before you attach the lining.

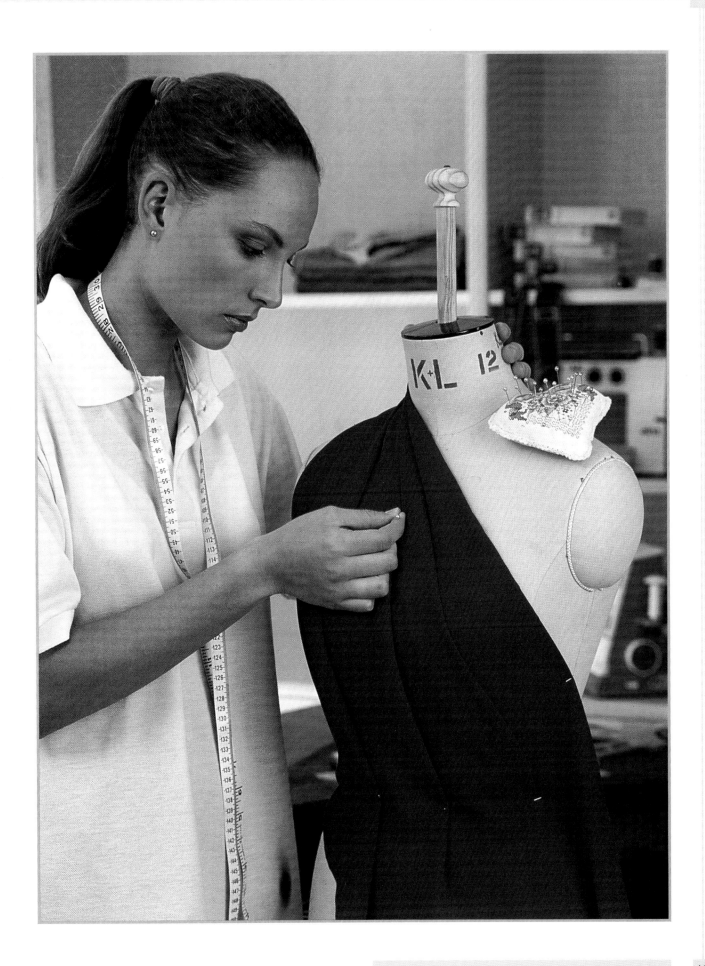

CONSTRUCTION 139

BLOUSE

Integrating industrial and dressmaking techniques will result in a good quality garment. When constructing a blouse or shirt, it is advisable to follow this assembly procedure in order to achieve a professional look. Although there is no right or wrong way, this step-by-step method is the simplest.

Prior to assembling the blouse, first prepare the collar, cuffs, pockets, buttonstands and any other extras. Finally, make the buttonholes and attach the buttons. Bear in mind that the focal points on a blouse are the collar and front placket, and therefore you should pay special attention to these.

A classic striped shirt

Trade tips

- Mark the grain lines correctly if you want to maintain the right drape.
- Buttonholes should be neat and clean. Trim away any excess threads or interfacing protruding from the buttonholes.
- If necessary, fuse both sides of the collar and collarstand with a lighter-weight interfacing to achieve a firm, smooth result. This will also prevent the seam allowances from shadowing, which can often be seen on lightweight fabrics.
- Fuse the cuffs in the same manner as the collars. This will balance the look. Topstitch close to the edge for a flat, finished effect.
- It is a good idea to press as you sew and at the completion of each operation.

'Luxury is not overt.
It comes in fabric,
colour, proportion –
things that last.'

Giorgio Armani

1 Select the desired blouse pattern and adjust or alter it if necessary, referring to the instructions given on pages 15–19.

2 Select the fabric and a compatible interfacing and conduct the all-important fuse test, as discussed on pages 24–25.

3 Lay up the fabric and then cut out the blouse, referring to the instructions given on page 26, pattern matching if necessary. Also cut out the corresponding interfacing.

4 Fuse the collar, collarstand, cuffs, buttonstand and any pocket facings required, referring to the appropriate instructions on pages 24–25. Press back any seam allowances.

5 Prepare the blouse as follows: stitch the collar (*see* page 100); stitch the cuffs (*see* page 129); stitch the buttonstand or the placket (*see* pages 69–83); stitch the sleeve plackets (*see* page 69); stitch any pockets (*see* page 131); sew any darts (*see* page 44); tack any tucks (*see* page 47). Overlock the edges where necessary.

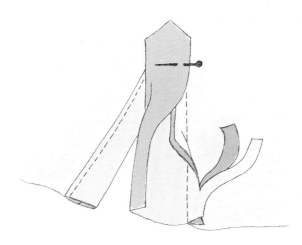

6 Attach the pockets as required. Assemble the yokes (*see* page 112) or the shoulder seams, and topstitch if required.

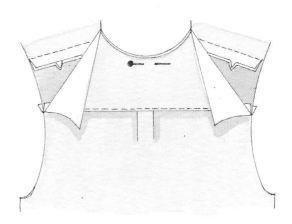

7 Attach the collar (*see* page 100); then the sleeves (using open method on page 122); then stitch the side seams, from the hem of the blouse to the sleeve hem; and then attach the cuffs (*see* page 129).

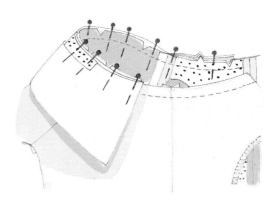

8 Stitch the hem, referring to page 59 and, finally, complete the buttonholes and attach the buttons as instructed on pages 76–83.

9 Trim off all unwanted threads and press.

WAISTCOAT

Waistcoats are usually worn to enhance the other garments in the ensemble. Take care when stitching even the smallest details, e.g. the buttonholes, as a waistcoat is often worn unbuttoned. Linings and facings can also become a decorative feature on a waistcoat. Very often, the back and fronts are cut in contrasting fabrics. This method of construction requires only a little handstitching.

Tapestry, brocade and other interesting fabrics are popular choices for waistcoats.

Trade tips

- Cut the lining 3 mm (⅛ in) smaller all round to prevent it from rolling to the outside. Alternatively, understitch or edgestitch the edges.
- Notch the lining and the waistcoat and align the appropriate notches to ensure that the lining fits onto the waistcoat when stitching.
- Be sure to stitch details, such as welt pockets, with unbroken lines of stitching.
- Trim and cut the buttonholes carefully to prevent jagged edges.
- Grade, trim and clip the seam allowances to prevent the edges from puckering, and then press to flatten them.

1 Establish the waistcoat fit desired and select the pattern accordingly (it may be fitted or loose). Adjust the pattern if necessary (*see* pages 16–18).

2 Select a suitable fabric and lining, and test interfacing to find one that is compatible with the fabric (*see* pages 24–25).

'Luxury need not have
a price – comfort itself
is a luxury.'

Geoffrey Beene

3 Lay up the fabric, cut out the waistcoat, pattern matching if required, and then do likewise with the lining. Cut the interfacing to correspond with the front facings (*see* page 26).

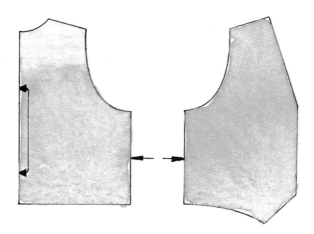

4 Fuse the fronts and the welts if necessary, and then insert the welts as instructed on page 136. If bound buttonholes are required, install them at this stage (*see* page 76).

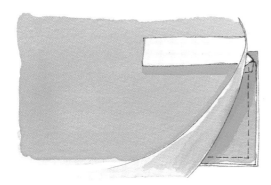

5 With the right sides facing, stitch the back and the front shoulder seams together. Press the seam allowances open. Repeat this procedure for the lining.

For eveningwear, print details can be highlighted with simple beading.

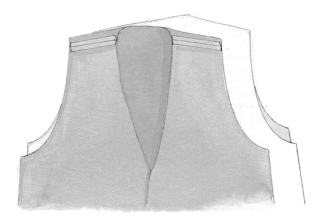

6 Position the waistcoat on the lining, with right sides facing and notches aligned. Pin and stitch from the side seam, along the hem, up and around the neck, and back to the side seam. Be sure to start and end about 10 cm (4 in) from the side seams.

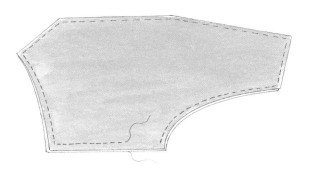

7 Trim the seam allowance to 3 mm (⅛ in) at the points. Turn the points right side out (refer to Corners, page 39). **NB Do not turn the rest of the waistcoat right side out yet.** Understitch the lining from the points at the hem to the neckline, sewing as far up the front as possible.

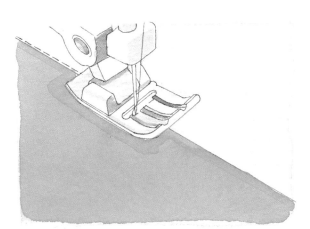

8 With the right sides facing, sew the lining to the waistcoat at one armhole, starting at the front and ending at the back. Trim the seam allowances. Repeat for the other armhole.

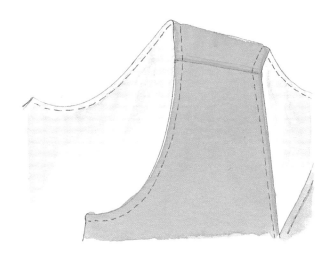

9 Reach into the waistcoat through the open side seam of one of the fronts, between the front waistcoat and the front lining and up through the shoulder, and then seize the back of the waistcoat. Should this be difficult, use both hands.

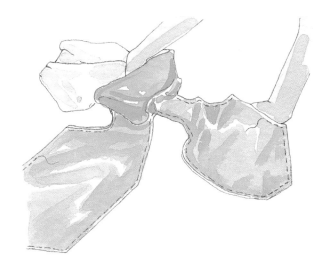

10 Pull the back gently through the shoulder and out of the open side of the waistcoat front. Repeat on the other side. Press the front and armhole seams carefully.

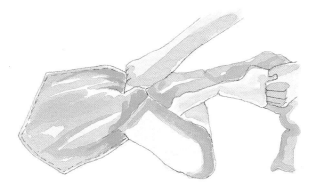

11 With right sides facing and notches aligned, pin the front to the back at one side seam. The waistcoat front and back will be joined and the lining front and back will be joined. Stitch one side seam together. **NB Do not sew the hem opening closed.** Repeat on the other side seam. Press the side seams towards the back.

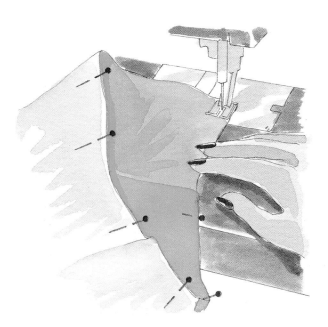

12 Turn the waistcoat wrong side out, but not the points. Pin the bottom of the waistcoat together, leaving about 10 cm (4 in) open at the centre back to turn the waistcoat right side out again. Stitch the hem at the back of the waistcoat on both sides of the opening. Press the seam line.

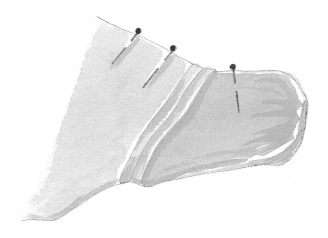

13 Turn waistcoat to the right side by pulling it through the opening at the centre back. Slipstitch the opening by hand. Press the edges using a pressing cloth. Mark and machine stitch the buttonholes and attach corresponding buttons.

UNLINED JACKET

Casual jackets are usually unlined and do not require the added support of extra interfacing as is the case with tailored jackets. They may have zipped fronts and banded hems, they may have cuffed sleeves, or they may even be collarless. The options are endless. The jacket discussed below is a zipped bomber-style jacket with cuffed sleeves.

Trade tips

- The zip weight should be compatible with the fabric weight, as should the choice of teeth, metal, nylon or polyester.
- To be assured of having a jacket with a uniform appearance, use the same interfacing for the collar, cuffs and waistband.
- Topstitching will help to flatten the edges of the jacket and it will also add quite a sporty look to the open-ended zip.

1 Select a suitable jacket pattern and adjust the fit if necessary.

2 Select an appropriate fabric and test the interfacing as instructed on pages 24–25.

3 Lay up the fabric, cut out the jacket, pattern matching if required, and cut the corresponding interfacing (*see* page 26).

4 Fuse the collars, cuffs, facings and waistband and any pocket pieces requiring interfacing. Press where necessary.

5 Prepare the jacket: stitch the collar (*see* page 100); stitch the cuffs (*see* page 129); stitch the pockets (*see* page 131); stitch the sleeve plackets (*see* page 69); sew any darts (*see* page 44); tack any tucks or gathers (*see* pages 47 and 53). Overlock where necessary.

6 Attach the pockets as required. Assemble the yokes (*see* page 112) or join the shoulder seams, and topstitch if required.

7 Attach the sleeves (using the open method on page 122), close the side seams and attach the cuffs (*see* page 129). Attach the waistband and insert the zip (*see* page 114) and the front facing. Attach the collar (*see* page 100). Overlock and press after each operation, where necessary.

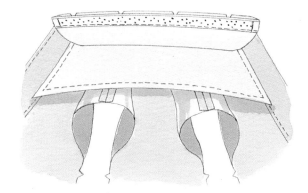

8 Stitch the buttonholes on the cuffs and attach the buttons. Trim unwanted threads and press.

RIGHT: This fabric is suitable for a soft jacket and does not require any lining.

LINED JACKET

Tailoring calls for the extensive use of interfacings to build up shape in the jacket. Complete garment sections are fused, and in some areas two layers of varying weights are used for distinctive effects. A partially tailored look can be achieved with less fuss by selecting a fabric with sufficient body and lining it correctly. This is the type of jacket constructed here. Following the correct sequence will simplify what appears to be an awesome task.

A satin trim adds definition to this evening jacket.

Trade tips

- Pre-shrink the fabric to prepare it for the extra steam used when fusing, and to prevent shrinkage.
- Accurate cutting, stitching, trimming, grading and pressing will result in a professional finish. Bevel trim the edges of heavy melton cloth to further reduce the bulk. Hold the scissors at an angle and skim the trimmed edges.
- Shorten the stitches around corners and outside curves where close trimming is required.
- Select a compatible lining that is lighter in weight and softer than the jacket fabric. The colour should also blend well with the fabric, and any printed lining must be selected with careful consideration.
- Fuse the hems of the jacket, as well as the sleeves and any centre back vents or pleats.
- It is advisable to make a test garment to check the fit prior to cutting expensive fabric. Check that: fronts hang straight without spreading open; vertical seams hang perpendicular to the floor; shoulder seams lie on top of the shoulder, without pulling to the front or back; set-in sleeves are smooth with rounded heads, no diagonal wrinkles in the sleeve and the sleeve does not pull across the upper arm; collar hugs the neck without gaping or wrinkling; lapels hug the bustline without gaping when buttoned; back vent hangs straight without spreading open across the seat; hem is straight; and jacket fits comfortably over the clothing intended to be worn with it.

1 Select a suitable jacket pattern, make up a test garment and follow the checklist given in Trade tips. Make the necessary adjustments to the pattern (*see* pages 17–18).

2 Select the fabric and test for a compatible interfacing as shown on pages 24–25.

3 Lay up the fabric, cut the jacket, pattern matching if required, and then cut the corresponding interfacing (*see* page 26).

4 Fuse the collar, facings, pocket openings, pockets, sleeve and garment hems, as well as any other sections that require support. Press back the seam allowances where necessary.

5 Stitch and attach the pockets (*see* page 131), and sew bound buttonholes at this stage if required (*see* page 78).

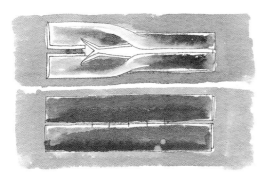

6 Join the shoulder seams and attach the notched collar (*see* page 102).

'The key to all design is an interest in fabric.'

Giorgio Armani

7 Stitch the side seams of the jacket and the seams of the sleeves. Easestitch the sleeve head and draw up the thread so that the notches of the sleeve and armhole match. Secure the ends, shrink out the excess with a steam iron and then pin the sleeve back into the armhole.

8 Stitch and press the sleeve head seam allowance only, up to 3 mm (⅛ in) beyond the seam line into the head. This will prevent the head from flattening. Do not press the underarm. Trim the underarm seams to 6 mm (¼ in).

For a professional touch, add a sleeve pad to support the sleeve head and prevent the seam allowance from showing on the right side. Cut a bias strip of lambswool, heavy flannel or fleecy non-woven fabric, 5 cm x 23 cm (2 in x 9 in). Fold 1.5 cm (⅝ in) from one long edge and align the folded edge with the sleeve head seam line, so that the wider side faces the sleeve. Slipstitch the folded edge to the sleeve seam.

11 Stitch the lining sections together, including the sleeves. Reinforce the armhole seam with two rows of stitching. Fold and machine tack the centre back pleat at the top and bottom of the lining. Staystitch the neckline, sleeve and bottom edge of the lining, and clip the seams at the neck.

9 Pin a shoulder pad into the garment so that it extends 12 mm (½ in) beyond the seam line. Fit the jacket and adjust the pad, if necessary. Attach to the shoulder seam by hand, using loose stitches, and tack the lower edge of the pad to the armhole seam. Do not stitch through all the layers of the pad.

12 With right sides together, stitch the lining to the facing of the jacket, starting and ending double the hem depth away from the bottom edge. Clip the seams at the curves and press the seams as they are stitched.

10 Hem the sleeves and the jacket according to the instructions on page 59.

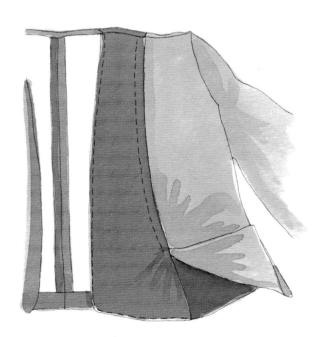

A lightweight classic jacket

A tweed hacking jacket

13 Match the seam allowances of the lining and the jacket at the shoulder and the underarm seams, and then tack in place. Lightly press the facing/lining seam allowances towards the lining, using a pressing cloth.

14 Trim the raw edges and hem the sleeve and jacket linings as instructed on page 59.

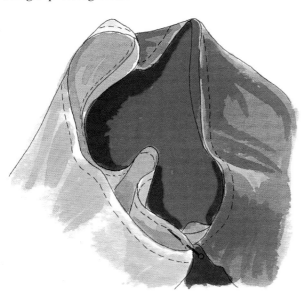

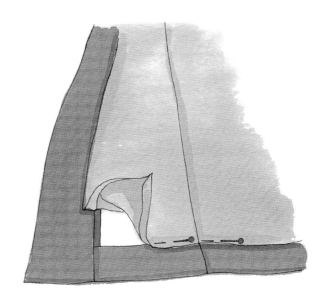

UNLINED SKIRT

The drape of the garment is the most crucial focal point in the construction of a skirt. For this reason, you must adhere to the grain lines. Other important areas where you should take care are the hem, the zip, the seams and the waistband closures.

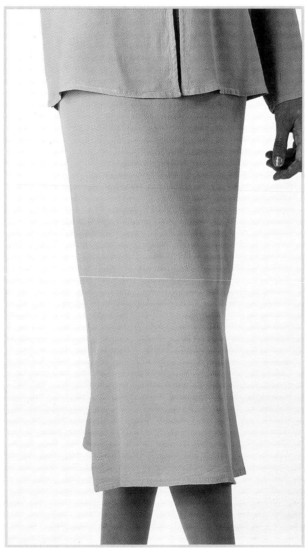

A mid-calf soft skirt

A casual mini skirt knotted at the waist

Trade tips

- Ensure that the hem hangs evenly and that it is in proportion to the fullness of the skirt. Straight skirt hems should not be wider than about 5 cm (2 in), whereas the width of a full skirt hem could be anything from about 2.5 cm (1 in) to as narrow as a rolled hem.
- Bias cut skirts can stretch out. It is imperative to allow the skirt to hang, at least overnight, before trimming the hem straight.
- Preferably attach waistband fasteners by machine, or else with small hand stitches.
- When stitching, apply slight pressure to the seam on either side of the needle in order to prevent puckers and ensure a smooth seam. Do not, however, apply any pressure to bias cut seams. This will only stretch out the seams, which will cause a rippling effect.

1 Select a suitable skirt pattern and adjust the fit if necessary (*see* pages 15–19).

2 Select an appropriate fabric for the skirt and then test the waistband and any other areas for a compatible interfacing, as instructed on page 24.

3 Lay up the fabric, cut the skirt, pattern matching if required, and then cut the corresponding interfacing (*see* page 26).

4 Fuse the waistband and any other required pieces (*see* pages 24–25).

5 Prepare the skirt: stitch any darts (*see* page 44); stitch any tucks (*see* page 47) or gathers (*see* page 53) on the skirt or separate frills, and draw up to match the notches; stitch any pockets (*see* page 131); and pleat where required (*see* page 49). **NB Hem prior to pleating.**

'Excess is always a
mistake.'

Giorgio Armani

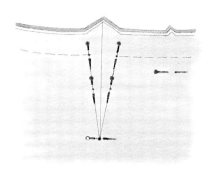

6 For open seams, overlock all the raw edges. Stitch the centre back or other seam requiring the zip. Attach the zip as instructed on page 84.

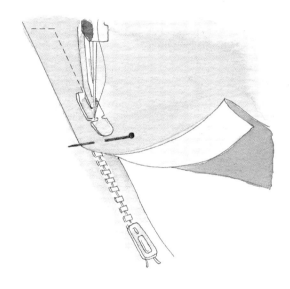

7 Attach any pockets (*see* page 131) and stitch the remaining seams. Attach any frills, then finish and trim the edges.

8 Attach the waistband (*see* page 114). Finally, hem the skirt (*see* page 59), stitch the buttonhole/s (*see* page 76), and sew on the button/s. Press.

LINED SKIRT

Lining a skirt is easy to accomplish. Any skirt can be lined, and by doing so, more body is given to the skirt, resulting in a professional appearance. Few patterns include a separate lining for the skirt. Simply use the skirt pattern and adjust the length. The hemline of the lining should be about 2.5 cm (1 in) above the skirt's hemline. A free-hanging slip lining is the simplest and, because it is only attached at the waist, it facilitates ironing by allowing you to lift the whole lining out.

Trade tips

- For a gathered skirt in a lightweight fabric, treat the fabric and lining as one layer of fabric.
- Unless the skirt is particularly tight fitting, it is not necessary to stitch down the darts; replace the fullness by stitching tucks.
- Unless the fabric frays badly, it is not necessary to finish the edges of the seams.
- Assemble the skirt before attaching the lining.

The construction for a dress is similar to that of a blouse and skirt. For a one-piece dress, follow the blouse sequence. For a shirtwaister, complete the blouse section and then the skirt section and, instead of attaching the waistband, attach the top to the skirt.

LEFT: The fabric is lined to add body to this wrap skirt.

1 Follow steps 1 to 7 for the unlined skirt (*see* page 153), cutting the lining simultaneously when you are cutting the skirt fabric.

2 When the skirt is darted, the lining will have corresponding tucks. Stitch the darts/tucks of the lining and then assemble the lining. Pin the corresponding seams and darts/tucks of the lining to the fabric. Alternatively, if the skirt is gathered, pin and attach the lining before gathering the skirt. Gather the skirt and lining simultaneously.

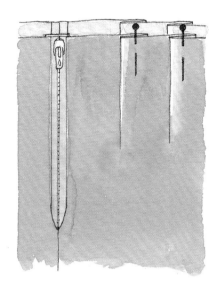

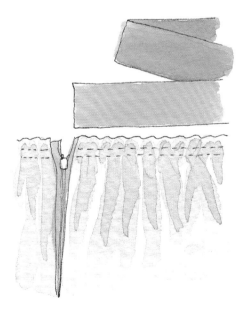

3 Turn to the wrong side and attach the lining to the zip tape. Alternatively, slipstitch by hand. Attach the waistband (*see* page 114).

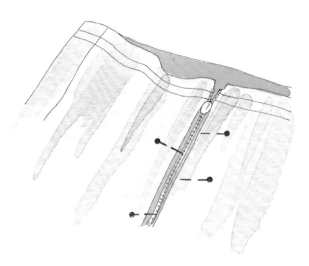

4 Hem the skirt and then the lining (*see* page 59) and press. Stitch the buttonhole (*see* page 76) and attach the button.

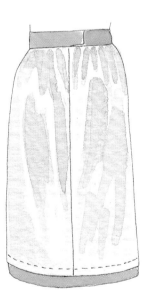

TROUSERS

Constructing a pair of trousers involves many techniques previously discussed. If assembled in the right order, the task will not be as daunting as it first appears. Areas that require special attention are the fly, pockets, pleats, front crease and waistband. To avoid puckering, interface the fly pieces on lightweight fabrics. Be sure to allow enough ease for the trousers to hang attractively on the body. The most important rule to follow is to cut the panels on the grain line, i.e. perpendicular to the hem, to prevent the side seams from twisting. Follow the same assembly procedure for shorts.

Trade tips

- Pleats should only be pressed flat above the crotch. It is preferable to position the pleat so that it merges with the crease line.
- Traditionally, pleats are folded towards the side seam. However, when folded towards the centre front, a slimmer effect is created.
- Pocket openings should be smooth and not stretched out. Interface the opening and add about 1 cm (⅜ in) to the length of the opening at the side seam, easing off into the side seam. This does not bulge out as would seem to be the case; it merely prevents the opening from pulling tightly across the hip.
- Always make sure that you match the grain line of the fabric with that of the pattern. This is crucial to the drape of the trousers.
- When stitching, apply slight pressure to the seam on either side of the needle in order to avoid rippling and puckering.
- Hems should not be wider than 2.5 cm (1 in) and may be slightly angled to the back.
- An alternative method of taking a crotch measurement is to measure from the front waist through the legs to the back waist.

> When no zip is required on the trousers, stitch the front and the back crotches separately, join the side seams and then join the inside leg seams, applying the same rules set out above.

LEFT: Classic pleated trousers

1 Select a suitable pattern for trousers and adjust the fit if necessary (*see* pages 17–19).

2 Select an appropriate fabric and test interfacing on the waistband and pockets for compatible qualities (*see* pages 24–25).

3 Lay up the fabric and cut the trousers, pattern matching if required. Cut the interfacing accordingly (*see* page 26).

4 Fuse the waistband, the pockets and any other necessary areas (*see* pages 24–25).

5 Prepare the trousers: stitch any darts (*see* page 44), tucks (*see* page 47) or gathers required (*see* page 53); stitch the pockets as instructed on page 131, topstitching where necessary.

6 Overlock all the necessary edges and stitch the fly as instructed on pages 88–90.

7 Stitch the back crotch seam and overlock the edges. Press. Join the side seams, aligning the notches. Overlock the edges, press, and topstitch where necessary. Join the inside leg seam, aligning the notches and the crotch seams. Stitch a continuous seam from the hem on the one leg to the hem on the other leg. Overlock the edges and press.

Belt loops made from spaghetti (rouleau) tubing or bias binding look decidedly home-made. Establish the number of loops required and multiply that by the width of the waistband plus 3 cm (1¼ in). This allows for 1 cm (⅜ in) seams and 1 cm (⅜ in) ease per loop. Cut the width 3 cm (1¼ in). Overlock one long edge and fold the strip in thirds, with the overlocked edge on top. Press flat. Topstitch 3 mm (⅛ in) from both folded edges. Cut the running strip into the number of loops required.

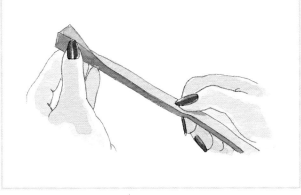

8 Make the belt loops (*see* box above) and attach to the waistline at the appropriate positions.

9 Stitch the waistband and attach to the waistline (*see* page 114). Stitch the belt loops in place at the top of the waistband and bartack to secure.

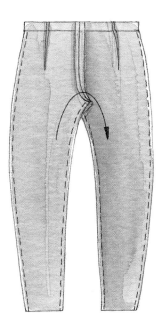

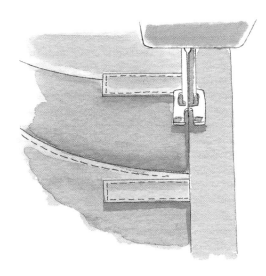

10 Hem the trousers (*see* page 59) and stitch the buttonhole and button in place (*see* page 76). Press the crease, aligning the side seams.

GLOSSARY

Breakpoint A point at the centre front edge where the revers starts to fold back.

Notch (vb) Cutting wedges from the seam allowances using a notcher.

(n) Symbols that are transferred from patterns to fabrics to indicate matching points.

Placket A garment opening fastened with a zip or buttons.

Revers The lapel (of a jacket or blouse) which is an extension of the garment front edge.

Roll line The line from the breakpoint to the shoulder on which the revers folds.

Slash A cut or slit made in a pattern to facilitate a construction. When slashing, make sure that you stop cutting just before the end of your mark so that all the pieces of the pattern remain attached together. This will guarantee accuracy in further construction.

INDEX